A *complete* guide to canine sports

The Really *Active*

Dog Book

Edited by **Julia Barnes** with contributions from:

Sue Garner · **Patsy Parry** · **Nicky Hutchison** · **Richard Curtis**
Lee Gibson · **Bridget Leek** · **Wendy Beasley** · **Lowri Davies**

ACKNOWLEDGEMENTS

The publishers would like to thank the following for help with photography: Sue Garner, Lee Gibson, Richard Curtis, Nicky Hutchison, Steve Nash, Keith Allison, Steph Rendall and The Swifts Flyball Team, MDS Ltd./Alvah (Flyball equipment), Bambury and District Dog Training Club (Carla Nieuwenhuizen, Anne Shepherds, John Simpson, Pat Sunderland, Di Assheton-Bowtle, Paul Thornton, Diana Stephens), Cornwall branch of the British Association of German Shepherd Dogs; Phil Dixon (www.culpeppers.co.uk), Anne Alderman and Bassett Allsorts Flyball Team (BFA Champions & Record Holders 2009), www.kisi.co.uk and www.snowpawstore.com.

Many thanks also to PoliceK9/Eden Consulting Group for the picture on page 116, and to Hill's Pet Nutrition for use of some of the illustrations from their *Atlas of Veterinary Clinical Anatomy* on pages 133 and 134. Page 129 © istockphoto.com/Justin Paget; page 131 © www.istockphoto.com/Sirko Hartmann.

THE QUESTION OF GENDER
The 'he' pronoun is used throughout this book instead of the rather impersonal 'it', but no gender bias is intended.

First published in 2010 by The Pet Book Publishing Company Limited
PO Box 8, Lydney, Gloucestershire GL15 6YD

ISBN
978-1-906305-35-2
1-906305-35-8

Printed and bound in Singapore.

CONTENTS

WHY TRAIN YOUR DOG?

Chapter 1

W hen a dog comes into your life, you need to have a vision of what you want and what your dog needs. Is your aim to have a well-behaved pet that will share your home, enjoy walks and other outings, and become an integral member of your family circle? Or do you have ambitions to compete with your dog in a chosen sport, and maybe bring home a dazzling array of trophies and rosettes?

Both goals are equally valid, but perhaps the one in the middle – where you simply enjoy training your dog so you can spend quality time together – is the most valid of all.

Working with your dog can build up a real bond.

What are the benefits of training your dog?

- **Mental stimulation:** Dogs are intelligent animals and love to learn. A bored dog is far more likely to turn to crime, as he has no other opportunity to use his brain.
- **Building a bond:** If you want a close relationship with your dog, you need to interact with him so he sees you as the focal point of his world.
- **Obedience:** Every dog should reach a basic level of obedience in order to be a good canine citizen.
- **Fitness:** In many of the sports, your dog needs to build up a level of fitness, which will improve his general health and well-being.
- **Having fun:** Not to be underestimated. You want your dog to respect you, but having fun is an important part of building a good relationship.
- **Achieving goals:** In every sport there is a ladder of achievement, and it can be hugely rewarding to see just how far you and your dog can progress.

EARLY TRAINING

It is never too early to start training – even if your dog will not be ready to compete until he is a fully mature adult. The aim is to build a good foundation that will get you off to a flying start when you start more specialised training.

When a puppy first arrives in his home at around eight weeks of age, he may look like a cuddly toy – but, remember, there is brain in there! A young puppy will soak up new experiences like a sponge and will use every waking minute to learn about the world around him. From the moment he arrives home, you should be showing your pup the behaviour you want and making it clear when behaviour is undesirable.

Set aside a few minutes every day to teach your dog basic obedience exercises, as these will be the foundation for later learning. As your dog matures, you can ask for more. But do not be in too much of a rush. Some dogs take longer to grow up than others, and if you put too much pressure on a youngster, you may permanently damage his ability – and his desire – to learn.

WHY SHOULD YOUR DOG CO-OPERATE?

In the following chapters, you will get an overview of the exciting canine sports that are available, and you can work out what is most likely to suit you and your dog. But you also need to get inside your dog's head and figure out what will motivate him to co-operate with you. Your dog does not *need* to learn how to negotiate an A-frame, perform a dance routine, or execute a lightning-fast turn from a flyball box, so why should he do as you ask? The question can be answered in one word – reward.

When a dog has learnt the skills of a particular sport, he will find great reward in carrying out the tasks that are required. But he also needs a more tangible reward – particularly when he is learning – so that he is motivated to keep on trying. When a dog is rewarded for a behaviour, he will repeat it so that he gets rewarded again. The more he is rewarded, the more he will want to co-operate. There are many ways to reward dogs – the trick is to find what is best for your particular dog (see page 8).

A dog has to be motivated to perform a given task.

A food treat is a tangible reward that most dogs will be ready to work for.

A game with a toy allows you to interact with your dog and reward him at the same time.

FOOD TREATS

Generally speaking, the way to a dog's heart is via his stomach, and giving food rewards will be effective in most training situations, and with most dogs. There are some breeds, such as Labrador Retrievers, who think that starvation is near at hand, and they will work with huge enthusiasm for the most boring of treats – a dry biscuit is a cause of huge excitement.

Other dogs are more picky, and they will only be motivated to work if you are offering a treat that is really special. Favourite treats include cheese, sausage, and cooked liver.

Get the most out of training with treats by observing the following rules:

- Unless your dog is a complete glutton, find out what type of treat really excites him. The dog will make his feelings crystal clear!
- Some dogs need maximum motivation, and you will need to use top-value treats for every training session.
- Most dogs respond to 'graded' treats. You can use a low-value treat (biscuit, dried food) for exercises he knows, and reserve your best treats (cheese, sausage or liver) if you are training a new exercise.
- Vary the treats while you are

training. Your dog will be more motivated if he gets a top-value treat for excellent work. It will encourage him to put in extra effort.
- If your dog has been struggling to learn a new exercise and then 'gets it', give him a jackpot treat – a small handful of treats – so that he gets a big reward for his hard work.

FAT DOGS

Treats – especially top-value treats, such a cheese and sausage, which are high in fat – are likely to pile on the pounds. Unless you are careful, your dog will become overweight. Obesity is a major problem and could shorten your

A dog will also respond to being stroked and given verbal praise.

TRAINING TIP

It may be that your dog works better for a toy than a food treat – or vice versa – but that doesn't mean you can't swap over to introduce some variety. Obviously, your dog will need to have some interest in a toy, which is something you can build up over a number of training sessions.

Keep the preferred reward when training new exercises, but, at other times, you can break up training sessions with a game or with a tasty treat.

dog's life. You will also find that a fat dog is dull and lethargic and will not want to work for you.

If you are planning a training session, cut down on the amount you are feeding at mealtimes on that day. It is also a good idea to go to your vet and get your dog weighed. If the vet considers that your dog is the correct weight, make a note of it. Then, get into the habit of weighing your dog every couple of months so that you will know if his weight has crept up and can take appropriate action.

TOYS
There are some dogs that are toy mad – and for them the greatest

reward is a game with their toy. Working Sheepdogs and Border Collies will often work better for a toy than for a food reward, and terriers also get focused on tug toys and Kongs. It is a matter of observing your dog and finding out what is most exciting for him – a toy or a treat.

If you opt for toy training, select a toy your dog really likes, and keep it especially for training. If the toy is not freely available, it will have added value in your dog's eyes, and he will work even harder for his reward.

PLAY CONTROL
A dog that is obsessed with his toy can get carried away with

enthusiasm very easily. He may get possessive over his toy and try to run away with it. Worse still, he may be resentful if you try to take the toy from him.

Right from the start, make it clear that the toy belongs to you, and you have control over it. Never let the dog grab the toy from you, and make sure you decide when to end a game.

PRAISE
Do not forget that praising your dog by word, or by touch, is a powerful reward. A dog that is working for you loves to be told how clever he is, and to be stroked and petted. This type of reward is unlikely to be enough

A dog will pick up signals from your body language.

on its own – particularly when you are training a new exercise – but it should not be underestimated.

COMMUNICATING
You have worked out what reward to use, but have you thought about how to communicate with your dog? Basically, you have two tools you can use: your voice and your body language.

USING YOUR VOICE
You need to be aware of how your voice sounds when you are training. It is all too easy to concentrate on the exercise, and issue commands like a sergeant major. Think of it from your dog's point of view: would you prefer to work for someone who barked out instructions, or for someone who made everything fun and exciting? You also need to guard against sounding boring and monotonous, otherwise the dog will simply switch off.

Try to keep your voice warm and encouraging – it doesn't matter how daft you sound – and when the dog does something right, sound as if all your birthdays have come at once! You want the dog to think he is having one big play session with his favourite person and the best thing in the world is to win your praise.

BODY LANGUAGE
Dogs are finely tuned to reading body language, and this can be used to our advantage in the following ways:

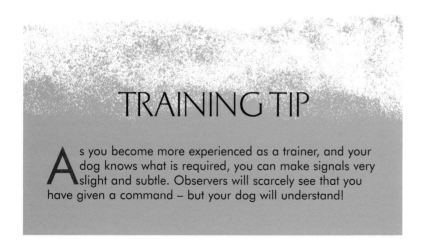

TRAINING TIP

As you become more experienced as a trainer, and your dog knows what is required, you can make signals very slight and subtle. Observers will scarcely see that you have given a command – but your dog will understand!

- **Reward:** A dog will see from your body language when you are pleased, and you can work at this by calling the dog in to be rewarded – with a toy, a treat, or simply a stroke. Keep your body open and welcoming, with arms outstretched, so that your dog knows he has done well and is coming to you for a big fuss.
- **Signals:** A dog will pick up signals from your body. This may be as simple as following hand signals, or he may watch the turn of your shoulders to see which direction you are going in.

GETTING IT WRONG

There are times when your dog makes a mistake and you need to correct him. You don't want to tell him off and dampen his enthusiasm, but you want to make it clear that his behaviour was incorrect so that he doesn't keep repeating it.

In the old-fashioned school of training, dogs were handled more harshly, and a stern tone of voice, or a yank with a check chain, was considered perfectly acceptable. Now we have learnt more effective ways of training dogs, and punishment is regarded as totally non-productive.

If you want to correct your dog, the best weapon you have is to ignore the behaviour you don't like and to reward the behaviour you want. If the dog does something wrong, use a neutral tone of voice, and say "No" or "Try again" – and don't give him a reward for trying, or he really

A motivated dog that understands the task will be happy to work for you.

will get confused!

Repeat this a few times and you will soon find that the dog abandons the incorrect behaviour because it is isn't getting him anywhere. If necessary, go back a stage in training so that your dog has a better idea of what is required. When he gets it right, make sure he knows the difference and give a jackpot treat (see page 8) or have a longer play with the toy.

STRESS LEVELS

If you are using positive training methods, and giving rewards that your dog values, he should be a willing pupil. However, dogs can become stressed if they fail to understand what you want or if they are pushed too hard.

A happy dog will:
- Wag his tail constantly
- Be bright-eyed and alert
- Focus his attention on you

Signs of stress from a dog who is unhappy about training include turning his head away and licking his nose.

rethink. Training must be fun for you and your dog, and if your dog is clearly distressed, you need to question what you are doing. Ask yourself the following:

- Are the training sessions too long?
- Does the dog value his reward?
- Is the dog confused because my training is muddled?
- Am I asking for something that the dog finds especially difficult because of his physique?
- Is the dog unduly worried about what I am asking him to do?

Have a long, hard think, and make sure you get to the root of the problem. It may be a single factor that is to blame, or it may be a combination of scenarios that have caused the trouble. If you are struggling to find a solution – and you are still keen to carry on with a training programme – enlist the help of a professional dog trainer or behaviourist, who will be able to assess the situation objectively and may come up with some good advice. However, if your dog is clearly unhappy, abandon your training programme and be content with having a loving companion who has his own special ways – even if he is not a born competitor.

- Be eager for the next command
- Be over the moon when he gets his reward.

An unhappy dog will:
- Look away from you – or walk away from you
- Yawn constantly

- Keep licking his nose
- Put his head down and either avoid eye contact or look up at you
- Keep scratching at his collar

If you dog shows any signs of stress, it is time for a major

SUMMING UP
Training your dog and competing with him is immensely satisfying, and we are fortunate that there is

Enjoy the good days – and remember you will always bring the best dog home with you.

a variety of disciplines so you are certain to find one that suits you and your dog. But no matter how successful you are – or how much you want to reach the top – your dog's welfare must always come first. The question you must always ask is: "Is my dog fit, free from injury and enjoying his training?" If the answer is a resounding "Yes", there will be no stopping you! But remember, your dog is not a machine – and neither are you. You will have good days and bad days, but there is one certainty – you will always take the best dog home with you.

COMPETITION OBEDIENCE

Chapter 2

Everyone appreciates a well-behaved, well-trained dog. An obedience-trained dog goes beyond the usual levels seen for a well-mannered pet. The vast majority of dogs competing at obedience shows are pet dogs first and competition dogs second, but their owners have a passion to train their dog further and get great enjoyment out of it. The bond between owner and dog created through their training is far stronger than with a pet dog, both gaining so much more from the relationship. It's an ideal way to meet like-minded people from all over the country and have a great day out.

WHAT IS OBEDIENCE?

Obedience shows are where the dog and its owner (handler) complete a number of exercises in succession with control and precision. The exercises in obedience include: heelwork, recalls, retrieve, stay, sendaway, distant control and scent discrimination. An exercise is a series of predetermined movements that the dog must perform in collaboration with the handler. The number, and degree of difficulty of exercises performed, will depend upon the level at which the dog and handler are competing.

Obedience can be likened to a gymnastic competition where the athlete aims for the perfect 10 in each exercise, with points lost for untidiness and technical errors. Obedience is just that. Teams of dog and handler start with full points in each exercise with points deducted for any deviation from the judge's view of the perfect execution of each part of the test.

Obedience shows cater for the full spectrum of people. There are

In competition, a dog must perform a prescribed set of exercises with accuracy and precision.

those who work towards the highest awards, to those who simply enjoy the social event and training their dog. The advantage of obedience is that one show will offer something for everyone and provides an opportunity for those who may feel they want to achieve more to watch and learn from the most experienced and successful dogs and handlers.

WHERE ARE SHOWS HELD?

Obedience shows take place in many areas and host a variety of classes that cater for a range of abilities and experience. The venues may vary from outside in large parks and sports fields to inside large sports halls, equestrian centres and purpose-built show grounds. So competitors need to be prepared for all weather types and environments.

WHAT TYPES OF DOG TAKE PART?

Any dog can compete in obedience shows and, as long as the dog is healthy, he can compete with his handler to an old age. Those dogs from the working, pastoral and gundogs groups show the most potential for obedience, as they have an inbred working ability that can be channelled to meet the needs of obedience exercises. The most common breed of dog at obedience shows in the UK and Europe is the Border Collie, but Belgian Shepherd Dogs, German Shepherd Dogs, Golden and Labrador Retrievers, Shetland Sheepdogs and Rottweilers are

The Golden Retriever has made its mark in obedience, particularly in the USA.

also quite popular. The USA has a good representation of Golden Retrievers competing at the highest levels of obedience. All sizes of dog can be successful, with small breeds, such as the Jack Russell and Border Terrier, up to the larger Afghan Hound and Great Dane competing with reasonable levels of success, including first places.

All dogs must be well balanced and sociable with other dogs and people before they can be entered for competition. This pre-obedience training is best done when the dog is still very young, so as soon as a dog is inoculated, he should be taken to as many places as possible so that he grows up to be calm and confident in all situations.

Some of the utility and terrier breeds do not have sufficient

It is more of a challenge to compete with a breed such as the Staffordshire Bull Terrier, but why not have a go?

ability to concentrate and physically perform the exercises effectively. However, this should not prevent anyone who owns one of these breeds from gaining great enjoyment from obedience training and competition. The key element, vital to all, is that the dog is well controlled at all times to ensure both his safety and those of the other competitors while at an obedience competition.

WHO CAN COMPETE?

Almost anyone can aspire to compete at obedience shows. Those who attend and enjoy obedience competitions are from all walks of life, of any age, and across a wide spectrum of physical ability from able-bodied to those who, for example, are wheelchair users or have poor hearing.

WHAT TYPES OF SHOW ARE THERE?

To compete at most shows it is essential for a dog to be registered with the appropriate kennel club before he can be entered for competition. In Europe and the USA, only pedigree dogs may be registered and thus entered to compete in obedience competitions. However, in the UK the Kennel Club has an activities register for non-pedigree dogs, thus opening up obedience competitions to all dogs.

The ideal starting place is a small show held within another event, such as an agricultural show, village fete or some other fundraising event. Generally, the classes are simple and set for those with little or no experience.

Progressing from this, there is a variety of obedience competitions of different levels, held in their own right. These range from a limited event, where the number of dogs permitted to enter is restricted to, for example, a particular breed, those who reside within a defined distance from the event, or simply any dog up

to a maximum number per class.

The highest level of obedience competition hosts classes for the top competing dogs and their handlers vying for the highest honours, namely the title of Obedience Champion. These are, invariably, the largest and most prestigious shows.

In the UK, Crufts Dog Show is the pinnacle event for all obedience enthusiasts, Europe has the FCI (Federation Cynologique Internationale) World Championships in Obedience, and the American Kennel Club has its National Obedience Invitational Championships.

All shows operate under licence, which ensures compliance with the rules and regulations as set out by the kennel club of the country. This ensures a consistent standard of organisation and safety, including the content of classes scheduled and who is qualified to judge the dogs.

All hold a range of classes catering for the least experienced dog and handler to those with a wide experience and a history of success, who have made progress through the various classes to compete at higher levels.

HOW DO I GET STARTED?

The absolute essentials before any dog can compete are for it to be:
• Physically fit and healthy
• Under good control at all times
• Of sound temperament with people and dogs
• A good traveller and happy to settle in the car at any time.

For any training session to be effective, the right reward must be found to motivate the dog. This could be food, something tasty and easily eaten. Most common food treats are: chicken, cheese, sausage, or homemade treats (such as liver cake or tuna cake). There is also a wide choice of training treats sold in pet stores. For some dogs, a favourite toy is just as effective. The 'selfishness' of dogs means they will do nothing just for the sake of it – but they will do almost anything for something they want. If an action/behaviour produces enjoyment and gives the dog great reward, then he will do it again.

To begin with, training sessions are best kept short and motivational to help teach concentration and not overstretch the dog. Training 'little and often' is a good regime to follow, especially with a young dog. Sessions can then gradually increase in both time and expectation, with the dog doing more for each reward. Never allow the dog to become confused or stressed. A good handler learns to read their dog; they understand the dog's reactions to various stimuli and so will tailor their training to suit the dog's temperament and ability, and to maintain the required level of concentration.

For all training, always ensure your dog understands one element of an exercise before moving on to the next. It is always best to ensure that a dog fully understands the basic training of any exercise before

Find a reward that your dog really wants to work for.

adding more complex work. A good trainer will always check a dog's basic knowledge and understanding throughout his competition career, so keeping a firm foundation on which all training is based.

WHAT WILL I ACHIEVE?
Most dogs are taught through play, creating the desire to work and building the confidence needed to go further. Dogs really love to work; it gives them a great rapport with their handler, which cannot be gained in any other way. Training will result in:
Great enjoyment for both dog and handler

- A strong relationship between handler and dog based on mutual trust and respect
- A more responsive dog in all situations
- An ideal means of relaxation and exercise
- An opportunity to meet many like-minded people
- Enhanced understanding of how dogs and humans communicate, and how to achieve more from it
- A means of keeping your dog both mentally and physically stimulated and fulfilled
- A tremendous pride in your dog
- Prizes!

Training classes range from basic pet obedience to those that specialise in competition obedience.

WHERE CAN I GO FOR TRAINING?

A dog learns by repetition, using simple commands and simple actions, alongside lots of reward.

It is best to take a dog to training classes that use praise and reward and motivational training techniques to teach dogs the basic content of the obedience exercises performed in competitions. The content of the various class levels will give clear goals and standards to achieve while providing an introduction to the obedience exercises. Many training clubs hold a range of classes for those who wish to simply have a well-mannered pet to the more competitive minded. So even if you are not certain if obedience is for right you and your dog, you can attend the classes, see how training varies for the different levels, and decide for yourself.

From a foundation class for pet dog training, competition training can start in earnest with a dog of any age. However, it is worth bearing in mind that a young dog is likely to respond more readily and will need less retraining to eradicate undesirable habits.

WHAT DOES IT INVOLVE?

It is essential that potential obedience competitors understand the exercises that are included within the various classes at shows if they are to have any chance of success. These are explained here, but the best means of discovering and understanding the nuances of obedience is to see it 'live'. If there is a show nearby, take the opportunity to go and take a look. There will always be someone there willing to answer any questions and even give you a guided tour.

HOW IS OBEDIENCE JUDGED?

An appropriately qualified judge is appointed for each of the classes scheduled at the show. The judge plans and sets the test for that day, which must comply with the strict content guidelines laid down by the relevant kennel club. The judge will have a mental picture of the ideal performance of each exercise; the winning team of handler and dog will be the one whose performance is most like this image. So, although some elements of the test will vary from show to show, the basic content (number and type of exercises) is always the same. A caller steward is appointed by each judge to ensure that everyone is given the same instructions throughout the day.

Each test will comprise a set number of exercises for which points are allocated. The judge will then deduct points for any deviation from the ideal performance. Minor errors will result in minor deductions, but

The first step is to teach the correct heel position in a static pose.

The heel position must be maintained while the dog is on the move, initially on lead.

more serious errors will result in non-qualifying marks or even prevent the dog from competing further on that occasion.

WHAT ARE THE EXERCISES?

In obedience the 'working side' is on the handler's left, meaning the dog will always start and finish an exercise at the handler's left-hand side. The person competing with the dog may not be the registered owner and so is called the 'handler' – a term used in this chapter. (photo of dog sat at heel)

The basic exercises to be completed in obedience are set out below. However, depending upon the country, such as USA (American Kennel Club) and Europe (FCI), other exercises are included.

HEELWORK

Heelwork is the most difficult exercise to do well at the highest level. It has been likened to horse dressage, as it must be performed by the dog in a happy and natural manner, with poise from the handler and precision from both dog and handler. The dog's shoulder must be approximately level with, and reasonably close to, the handler's leg at all times when the handler is walking, maintaining a consistent position relative to one another. Any deviation from this is considered a fault with points deducted by the judge. Where the lead is attached for heelwork, it should be slack at all times.

As dogs naturally have an excellent ability to read body language, the handler's deportment is read by their dog so that when competing without verbal commands from the handler, the dog knows when to turn, change pace or stop. A

Heelwork starts with a basic pattern of straight lines and some turns.

successful team of dog and handler will communicate silently: i.e. no use of lead, no verbal commands or signals, the dog reading every nuance of the handler's movement. Those who teach their dogs these messages most effectively – and use them consistently – are the most successful competitors. These movements are quite obvious in the early stages of training, but they must be minimised as the dog gains experience. This avoids losing marks for excessive use of body signals due to poor deportment at the higher levels of competition.

Heelwork content will be set to the level of, and will include only those elements permitted for, that class. Generally, the handler and dog will be expected to move at a normal walking pace through a pattern of straight lines and turns. At a more experienced level, circles and weaves set by the judge and instructed by the caller steward are included. On paper a heelwork test can resemble a road map.

The classes for newcomers or 'Beginners' contain a fairly simple heelwork pattern executed with the lead attached and then with the lead removed. At this level, the handler is encouraged to verbally motivate the dog as much as necessary. As the class levels progress, the amount of support and instruction given to the dog by the handler is restricted, and the content of the heelwork test becomes more complex to include various parts carried out at different paces – fast, normal and slow – and more complex turning manoeuvres.

In the UK the heelwork exercise is a major part of the whole test, taking the most time to complete in comparison to the other exercises. This has developed over the years, along with an increasing desire for accuracy with style. It has somewhat less prominence in the USA and Europe where the length of pattern set is usually shorter.

The heelwork pattern becomes increasingly complex with minimal instruction from the handler.

Consistency is the key to achieving good heelwork: that is, consistent deportment, commands and overall training method. There is no set method to teach good heelwork, but whichever you chose, do not mix and match with other methods, as they may be incompatible.

It is best to break any exercise down into its constituent elements, teaching the basic elements initially and adding the more complex elements, such as turns and paces, later. Always ensure there is complete understanding of one element before moving on. Success comes with training, carried out in a consistent manner and with

empathy and understanding of the dog's ability to learn and concentrate.

Commonly, those who suffer least success do so because they are inconsistent, training in a way that does not ensure the dog has absorbed the basic elements before moving on. Many believe that once a dog has demonstrated something once or twice, he has learned what is required. This is most definitely not true and causes many errors seen in competition. A good trainer will always check that the dog fully understands what is needed and will often recheck later, even when competing at a much higher level.

RECALL TO HANDLER
This is similar to calling the dog back at the end of a walk, but instead of simply waiting until the dog is away from the handler, he is instructed to wait, either in a sit or down position. Then, after the handler has walked away, he is called to smartly come, sit neatly in front, and then instructed to go to the left-side heel position

As with all exercises, to teach this well it should be broken into its constituent elements: the wait, the call, the present, the finish. Each element is taught separately, and then only occasionally put together in training, especially in the early stages. Common errors

RECALL TO HANDLER

The handler leaves the dog in the Sit.

The dog is called in. Initially, the handler gives lots of encouragement.

The dog comes in to the Present position.

RECALL TO HEEL

The dog is left in a static position.

The hander recalls the dog to the heel position. The signals will become more subtle as the dog progresses.

Dog and handler continue with the heelwork pattern.

occur when the whole exercise is 'practised', rather than trained each time. The dog will then see only the finished product and anticipate elements such as the call and finish.

It is good to motivate the dog through play to recall as fast as possible, but this is easily lost if the reward for each element is removed too soon.

RECALL TO HEEL

Usually known as the class A recall. After leaving the dog in a sit or down position, the handler walks away from the dog. Then, on command, the dog is expected to move swiftly into the heel position and both dog and handler continue on together as in heelwork.

RETRIEVE AN ARTICLE OR DUMBBELL

The principles of this exercise are the same for all levels. At the beginner level the retrieve article can be anything chosen and supplied by the handler, then it must be a handler's own dumbbell at an intermediate level, and an article supplied by the judge at the higher levels. The judge must provide a similar, clean article for each dog entered on the day. It cannot be food, and it must be safe and suitable for all breeds of dog to pick it up. Examples include a piece of wood, rubber hose, washing-up brush, plastic container, knotted duster, or rolled up magazine – the possibilities are almost endless. Judges will, if necessary,

provide an article in various sizes, to cater for all the varieties of dog.

The dog must go directly and cleanly pick up the article, return to the handler, sit straight in front, release the article when the required and move neatly to heel.

The exercise must be taught carefully if it is to be performed well. Controlling each element is key. The recall, present and finish are all taught in the recall to handler training. The dog now has to learn to hold an object in its mouth at the same time.

It is best to teach the dog to hold a fairly soft article initially so that it does not cause the dog discomfort in his mouth. The dog must learn to open his mouth and gently take the article from

TEACHING RETRIEVE

To begin with the dog needs to learn to hold the article without mouthing.

In advanced classes, the judge will choose the retrieve article.

The dog must wait in position when the article is thrown.

The dog must run directly to the article and pick it up cleanly.

The dog returns to the handler.

The dog sits in the Present position.

The handler takes the article.

The dog is instructed to finish which means returning to the left-hand heel position.

Exercise finished.

your hand first, then from the ground. If the dog is allowed to become too excited during the training of the retrieve, it often results in an untidy execution of the exercise in competition. Progress training in small steps so that the dog gradually moves further from the handler to pick up the article, and then returns with it to sit neatly in front of the handler. Other retrieve items are introduced when the dog is confidently completing the exercise.

Controlled training prevents the common errors of 'mouthing' (when the dog constantly bites on the article rather than holding it firmly in his mouth), running on after pick up (rather than returning immediately), and pouncing on the article on pick up ('killing it').

SIT AND DOWN STAY

All classes have stay tests that require the dog to remain in the sit and down position without moving while the handler walks a distance away for a designated length of time, returns and releases the dog from the stay position. As the classes progress, the time of each stay test increases and the handler walks out of sight of the dog.

The basic stay exercises will comprise of a one-minute sit-stay and two-minute down-stay, the handler moving a few paces away from the dog. At the most advanced level, it is a two-minute sit-stay and a 10-minute down-stay with the handler out of sight of the dog.

STAY EXERCISE

A dog must be given the confidence to remain in the Stay – even when the handler is out of sight.

25

SENDAWAY

The judge sets up markers to designate the drop area.

The sendaway command is given.

The dog must proceed directly to the drop area.

The dog drops in the designated area and waits for the next command.

The exercise is finished with a recall to heel.

At all levels, once the dog has been commanded to stay, no further commands by the handler are permitted until the dog is released. Thus all dogs really need thorough training for this exercise. The dog must learn to sit or lie down first, then maintain the position without moving for increased lengths of time and with the handler further away, and eventually out of sight. A dog can feel vulnerable during the stay, so all stages of training must ensure the dog remains confident and at ease. Regular rewards for maintaining the stay work well. These are then gradually reduced so the dog remains in the stay position longer before a reward is given.

Many dogs fail this exercise when they have not been trained to maintain their concentration while remaining still, or have insufficient confidence to stay and so will move to be close to the handler. Others may simply decide to play with their neighbour!

SENDAWAY DROP AND RECALL
The dog, when instructed, must run in a straight line away from the handler, stop in either a sit or down position immediately on command at a designated point and then, when called to do so, recall promptly to heel.

It is usual for judges to use markers to set out the drop area. These can be any shape or size, and set in any pattern. Most commonly, a triangle of three or box of four markers is set up; the dog is then required to run into the area between the markers and drop into the down position. The judge will state where within the drop area they wish the handler to drop the dog.

Training will consist of a number of elements. The look command teaches the dog to focus in the correct direction and place. The stop will ensure a prompt response by the dog to the sit or down command. Incomplete training of these can often result in a complete failure of this exercise when under test.

DISTANT CONTROL
This is the most difficult exercise for the dogs to perform in obedience and so it is only included at the highest level of competition. The dog must

27

DISTANT CONTROL

The sequence starts with the dog in the Stand.

The next move is the Sit...

...followed by a Down. A further three moves are needed to complete the sequence.

execute six positions – a combination of stand, sit, and down – while the handler is up to 20 paces away. The dog must not travel more than a body length in any direction during the exercise. Only a verbal command or signal, used with the dog's name, is permissible to move the dog into each position. Training this exercise well takes time and perseverance to achieve confident, swift responses from the dog.

That said, with modern training methods, most dogs perform distant control well and it certainly looks quite impressive as a party trick!

As this exercise must be executed at a distance, many dogs have a tendency gradually to move towards the handler with each position. Training will teach the dog to move backwards, away from the handler, with confidence. There are a number of methods that will achieve this, but all involve each position taught beside the dog, then gradually at increasing distances away.

Care must be taken to teach one movement before adding others.

SCENT DISCRIMINATION

All dogs have a far superior sense of smell to humans, as their noses contain many more scent receptors – so, in obedience, we simply utilise the dog's natural ability.

In this exercise in the UK, the dog must initially find and retrieve the handler's scent on a cloth, supplied by the judge, and placed among a straight line of five other unscented (blank) cloths. Simply holding a cloth between the hands for a few moments provides sufficient scent for the dog to complete this exercise successfully.

Then a decoy cloth is introduced, and the number of cloths is increased to a maximum of 10 in any pattern. A decoy scent is provided by a person

SCENT DISCRIMINATION

The dog takes in the scent from the cloth.

He now works his way around the cloths.

A positive identification.

The dog picks up the cloth and heads back to the handler.

The cloth is presented to the handler.

TIPS FOR COMPETITION

- All dog training must be fun and exciting for both dog and handler. Obedience is no exception and can be great fun, without losing the elements of precision required.
- Training to achieve this follows a fine line. Step over and the dog is too enthusiastic in his work. On the other hand, the dog can be de-motivated and show no interest.
- It's essential to understand your dog's nature, whether it be sensitive, bold or excitable, as, with this knowledge, you will know how best to handle him and get the best responses in training and competition.
- Our training and how we teach our dog ultimately must resemble how we behave under a test situation, so body language and deportment must be consistent during training and then be mirrored when in competition.
- To be successful a handler must cope under pressure. The best competitors control their nerves, do not relay their apprehension to their dog, and maintain their concentration throughout the test.

- To achieve a competitive edge, trust the dog in his ability to perform. This is done through thorough training, especially of the basic elements. To train a dog to compete successfully takes many, many hours of training spread over the dog's whole career.
- Attend a good training class to guide you through all elements of training at the rate appropriate for you and your dog. It is here that guidance is given at each stage, hopefully preventing too many training faults before they become problems. It also provides the atmosphere so a dog learns how to cope with the distractions experienced at shows.
- You need a firm understanding of the requirements of each class, the individual exercises and the standard required.
- Before entering competitions, it is a good idea to spend time watching dogs under test at a variety of shows. Take on helping roles at a show, which is an excellent means to gain an understanding of the exercises and the nuances of competition.

unknown to any of the dogs competing in the class, who will also hold a cloth for a few moments at the same time as each handler. Both cloths are set out at the same time.

Finally, the dog must locate and retrieve the judge's scent on a cloth among both decoy and blank cloths. The judge will hold two cloths at once; one is given to the handler to show the dog,

and the other is placed in the scent pattern along with the blank and decoy cloths.

In Europe and the USA the scent articles are wood or leather, but the principles are the same.

All dogs have the basic ability to perform this test with ease. The aim of training is to channel basic ability. The key is to teach discrimination in order to find the familiar scent of the handler,

moving on to the unfamiliar scent of another person, the judge. When we consider the role of some dogs trained to seek out drugs or explosives hidden in many different places with many other scents to try to prevent detection, obedience scent discrimination is easy.

It is essential to have strong recall and retrieve exercises before commencing scent training. A good starting point is to ask the dog to find something such as a toy or fir cone in long grass while on a walk. This will teach the dog to use his nose on command. Then more formal training commences where the dog finds an article hidden among others too large to pick up in error. A gradual progression entails adding smaller non-scented items that the dog must ignore, then scented (decoy) items.

Common errors occur if the retrieve exercise is weak. A lack of training to teach the dog to discriminate one scent from another will allow the dog to pick up and drop blank sheets, or even retrieve decoy articles.

SETTING GOALS
Setting goals provides clear objectives and a measure for success. Anyone wishing to compete at the highest levels in obedience may have the ultimate goal of achieving the title of Obedience Champion for their dog or competing at Crufts dog show. Others may feel this is not for them so may merely wish to enter a show and complete the test.

A great deal of dedication is needed to maintain the high standard of training over a dog's entire career. Success is not time limited, so there is no need to rush your training.

Many who embark on an obedience competition career

The aim is to build a relationship of trust and reward so that your dog enjoys competing as much as you do.

with their dog may not have great expectations, but with success can come a desire to achieve more. Once bitten by the 'obedience bug', invariably the aim is not just to complete the test but to win and move to the higher levels of competition. This can ultimately result in gaining the title of Obedience Champion.

Naturally, not all dogs achieve this highest accolade, but this makes it even more precious. Understanding this, the saying: 'aim for the stars and maybe reach the moon' has a great meaning for obedience enthusiasts. A few lucky ones reach the stars (Obedience Champion), but quite a few reach the moon (the goal you set yourself).

WHERE CAN I FIND OUT MORE?
The kennel clubs around the world provide information of all dog training societies and individuals registered with them who host obedience classes and obedience shows. They can also provide information on registration requirements. Visit the website www.thekennelclub.org.uk for the UK, www.akc.org for the USA and www.fci.be for Europe.

Many vets and pet stores also provide information about dog training classes in their area. They inevitably see the results of those who attend and so will know which achieve the best results. Never be afraid to take a look at a class before you enrol – this way your dog is not exposed to an unsuitable class.

If you see someone training their dog in a manner you wish to follow, simply ask them where they attend classes. Many are only too happy to provide you with the information.

Obedience training will give you and your dog years of enjoyment together. If you ever get to the dizzy heights of competing at and actually owning an Obedience Champion – Wow!

But never let ambition rule your heart or your head. Your dog is first and foremost a companion, and should always be loved and valued for this role rather than for the trophies you bring home.

RALLY O

3 Chapter

Rally O is a new sport in the UK, but is becoming increasingly popular. It is loosely based on obedience but is more relaxed than competitive obedience, and also has a few exercises borrowed from the sport of agility when you get to the higher levels. The sport has its foundations in America, with the American Kennel Club (AKC) and the American Association of Pet Dog Trainers (APDT) each having their own versions of the sport. Canada, Slovenia and other countries enjoy Rally O, and the UK is now developing its own version.

Because it is still in its infancy, changes to the rules and exercises are inevitable. The details in this chapter are the ones currently in use, but, as the sport matures and new organisations take over control, they will undoubtedly develop different exercises, rules and scoring criteria – so check with your local Rally O organisation before entering a competition.

Currently, Rally O has a total of 55 exercises over the three levels, plus bonus exercises. A course will have between 12 and 20 exercises in it.

HOW IT STARTED

Rally O was the brainchild of Charles (Bud) L. Kramer, who was also the innovator for the first American agility programme, back in 1984. Rally O was officially launched in the USA in 2005. Bud – a long-time obedience competitor – noticed that entries to traditional obedience competitions were in decline and wanted to find something new and exciting for dogs and owners to compete in.

He developed the idea of Rally O where the major objective is for the dog and handler to work as a team, with attitude being at least as, if not more, important as precision. Owners are allowed to talk to their dogs as they work, encouraging them with their voice, and, in level one, by patting their legs or clapping their hands. Owners are not allowed to physically touch their dogs or feed them while working, but verbal and visual encouragement is expected.

Rally O is open to any breed or type of dog, and owners and/or dogs with disabilities are actively encouraged to take part, as long as the dog does not show signs that it is in pain when working. If an owner needs to modify the completion of an exercise – to allow for their disability – they provide the judge with details before the competition starts.

Any owner who wants their dog to behave at home, in the company of other dogs and

Rally O is a more relaxed form of obedience competition where dog and hander work round a course, completing a variety of different exercises.

public places – but who also wants to teach him to do a bit more than the basic exercises – will enjoy training for Rally O.

Thankfully, harsh verbal and physical corrections are not allowed in Rally O and will result in marks being deducted, or disqualification from the round. This rule applies both in and out of the ring, with judges and representatives of the organisation watching for this at all times. Overly harsh handling will result in the owner being asked to leave the competition ground. The aim of rally is team building – working together without punishment or coercion. It is about the dog, owner and spectators having fun and encouraging owners and dogs to work as one.

WHAT IS RALLY?

The team of dog and handler perform exercises as in an obedience ring, but instead of a steward 'calling' the exercises, the team works round a numbered course (as in agility), with each numbered sign giving details of what is required. The dog works at the handler's left-hand side (unless an owner's disability means they are incapable of doing this), but a glued-to-the-owner's-leg type of heelwork is not required. Instead, the dog works on a loose lead (in level one), or off-lead (in levels two and three), in a position where the owner would be able to reach out their hand and touch the top of their dog's head. The owner should not have to look over their shoulder to see their dog, and neither should his mid-body be ahead of the owner, as this would be considered 'forging ahead' and would incur penalty points.

The judge sets up the course as he wishes and the handlers are allowed 10 minutes to 'walk the course' to familiarise themselves with the route and the exercises required, and to ask the judge any questions that might arise. The courses can be different at each trial.

The course is made up of 'stations' – numbered signs that

This type of competition is ideal for owners who want to train their dog to do more than the basic exercises – but do not want the pressure of competing in formal obedience.

tell the handler what exercise they need to perform – and each level has a maximum and minimum number of stations required to make a course. Although the rounds are timed and should be finished within four minutes, the team works around the course at their own pace.

Most exercises (e.g. sit, down, u-turn) are performed just in front of the station (within 2-4 ft/60-120 cm), although some exercises (e.g. moving side step right, jump and return to handler) are performed beside or after the sign.

The judge gives only one command – for the handler and dog to start their round. It is then up to the team to complete the round in the correct order.

Of course, as in any competition, there has to be a score. In Rally O UK you start with 100 points and each fault earns a deduction from this. The number of points deducted depends on the fault. For example, one point is deducted each time the lead (if used) goes tight or for a poor sit; three points are deducted if you have to re-try an exercise, and 10 points will be deducted if the exercise is not performed correctly.

The judge will watch as the team goes around the course, deducting points for faults as they occur and marking the reason on a score sheet. Some organisations will deduct points if the dog barks excessively; others will see this as

enthusiasm for the task and not penalise. Aggressive barking is a different matter, and a judge may excuse a team from the ring for unmanageable behaviour.

To pass, or qualify, at each level requires a minimum score of 70 points (i.e. less than 30 points deducted for faults). Each team – of handler and dog – must qualify at least three times before receiving a Rally O title, and moving on to the next level.

THE LEVELS
There are three levels that you will work your dog through:
- **Rally Level One – Novice:** This is performed with the dog on-lead. There are 18-20 exercise stations and there are no more than five stationary exercises. At this level,

It is a sport that is open to everyone, including owners and/or dogs with disabilities.

competitors may pat their legs and clap their hands to encourage their dog. The winning title is RN (Rally Novice).

- **Rally Level Two – Advanced:** This is performed with the dog off-lead and includes at least one jump. There are 12-17 stations, excluding the start and finish signs. The winning title is RA (Rally Advanced).
- **Rally level Three – Excellent:** This is for dogs who have earned their advanced title. It is performed with the dog off-lead and requires more precision and co-ordination between dog and handler. It will include at least two jumps over 15-17 stations. Physical encouragement is not allowed

at this level. The winning title is RE (Rally Excellent).

Titles can be earned at each level, and Championship titles can be earned by successfully completing three course runs with qualifying scores.

THE SIGNS
The signs may be any colour and will give descriptions (and directional arrows if appropriate) for each exercise. The signs are numbered to allow the handler to follow the course in the correct order. Most exercises are performed with the sign at the handler's right-hand side, but there are exceptions. They will be large enough to be recognised when following the course.

SCORING
The minimum deduction is one point, with deductions going up to 10 points. Dogs that bark excessively will receive deductions depending on the severity of the behaviour shown. A non-qualifying (NQ) score is the largest deduction. Handlers who are using food rewards may not enter the ring with food in their hands or have treat bags on display; food rewards must be kept in a pocket or left outside the ring.

GETTING STARTED
Before you enter a rally competition, your dog should know basic commands and pay attention to the handler. It is important that the dog can walk on a loose lead (as defined earlier) throughout the course.

WALKING TO HEEL

The heelwork position does not demand the precision of competitive obedience, but the dog should not forge ahead or lag behind. Handlers and dogs will be asked to walk in straight lines, execute turns, and change pace. There are also exercises that involve more complex patterns, such as figures of eight and serpentines.

Attentive heelwork is needed as handler and dog work their way around the course.

270-degree right turn.

Right turn.

Pivot right.

Slow pace.

Straight figure of eight with the dog weaving around the cones, still maintaining a good heelwork position.

STATIC EXERCISES

These exercises test basic obedience, with the dog responding to commands to go into different positions. In some of the exercises the dog must 'stay' even though the handler is moving.

The dog is asked to 'Sit' and must then go into the Down position.

The dog must stay in position
while he is circled by his handler.

RECALL EXERCISES

The Recall exercises are more advanced and combine static positions – Sit, Stand, Down – with a response to the Recall. The dog may also have to stay in position, as the handler leaves him.

The dog is called into the Front position.

The handler backs away as she calls the dog to her.

SUMMING UP

There are a wide variety of exercises in Rally O, but they are well within the capabilities of a well-trained pet dog. This sport is all about building a band with your dog and having fun. Hopefully you have read enough to consider giving this sport a go. Because Rally O is still in its infancy, you may have problems finding specific classes in your area, but don't let this put you off. Organisations such as the APDT in the UK run seminars and workshops that you may be able to attend – have a look on the internet for details.

In the meantime you can start preparing by going to a dog training class and teaching your dog basic cues/commands. You will need to teach him to sit, down, walk on a loose lead, wait, turn and all sorts of other things that will be taught at classes anyway.

The dog is left in the Sit

A good response to the "Come" command.

The dog must drop into the Down position as he reaches the handler.

Agility and Obedience are combined in this exercise. Firstly the dog is left in the Sit.

The dog is recalled.

A neat jump over the hurdle to return to the handler.

Make sure you practise all the basic exercises with your dog in various locations – in your home, in the garden, out on walks, in the park, at the training hall, at the woods – so he is able to 'generalise' his training and also learn to work with distractions.

All of these things will stand you in good stead when you find a Rally O class. And if you really can't find a class or seminar to go to, why not ask your training club to think about offering Rally O as one of its activities? It is bound to be popular, as lots of people enjoy working as a team

with their dog.

You will be able to download Rally O signs from the internet – make sure they are appropriate to the UK rules – and there are also books and videos available for you to learn more about the sport. Good luck and always remember: have fun!

CANICROSS

Chapter

F ive... four... three... two... one! Go! Welcome to canicross, the sport of running cross-country attached to your dog – or dogs!

Although canicross has only recently been recognised as a 'sport', man and dog have probably been running together in one form or another since they hooked up in the dim and distant past around prehistoric camp fires. Over the past 20 years or so – and most likely before that – competitive and recreational runners have got their dogs to join them on practice runs to exercise them and for the pleasure of their pets' company. Canicross has simply attached a lead to the dog and made it into a joint enterprise with the bias towards true teamwork.

It is a sport that can suit all types of dog owners: from adrenaline junkies who enjoying hurtling down muddy slopes with turbo-charged canines, to recreational runners and nature lovers who simply enjoy a bracing workout to stay fit and get some fresh air.

Most dogs love to run; it is an ideal outlet for all that canine physical energy without letting them get into mischief. Your dog is not going off doing his own thing but learning that you are fun to be with. If you teach canicross commands, your dog also has to use his brain, so it will meet all your dog's needs and help you to form the strong bonds that come from working with your canine pal.

If your dog is already involved in a working activity, canicross can help build strength and stamina that will give you the edge in other areas of your dog's life, such as in agility or gundog disciplines.

COMPETITIVE CANICROSS

You can canicross for the sheer pleasure of a shared activity to keep you fit, or you can train to compete. Races around country and forest trails, specifically for canicrossers, are run in Great Britain, Europe and USA and Canada. A variety of courses is usually on offer, from around 2.5 km to 7.5 km (1.5-4.6 miles), which is ideal if you are just getting going, although longer distances are also possible. Races can vary slightly in format, with European competitions favouring a 'mass' start where everyone sets off together. The mass start is spectacular, fun, exciting, and a bit hairy in all senses of the word. It certainly requires some skill and a well-behaved dog who is comfortable with his fellow canines.

Timed starts, where each runner leaves at set intervals and is timed against the clock, are

43

Canicross competitors can compete in specialist events or join in with fun runs.

favoured in the UK and are certainly more suitable for the cautious canine. The winners are obviously the fastest human-dog team around the set course. Most races have different categories depending on the age and gender of the canicrosser. These will include sections for junior, adult and veteran canicrossers; consult race organisers' rules to find out which category you should enter.

If you are keen to compete then probably the top canicross event is the World Dryland Championship, which is overseen by the International Federation of Sled Dog Sports and is held every year in a different country.

Most race organisers allow for only one dog, although British races also have a two-dog category for the seriously deranged dog runner. Do not try this until you have trained each dog individually and you know that you have the skills to control your dogs in all eventualities. Also ensure that the dogs concerned are evenly matched.

Races are generally well signposted with markers so you do not get lost. Trails also have marshals at set points, with watering opportunities for your dog and in case you get into difficulties. Runners with dogs that are struggling should stop running and consult a marshal, who can muster help from the on-site race HQ in the form of advice or off-road transport. Because of the shorter distances of most races, no rest stops are required and it will be up to individual runners to monitor their dog's condition throughout the race. Larger races may have a vet attending, or the central organisational point will have a noticeboard with the telephone number and address of the named on-call vet.

There are some human-only

running races that allow canicrossers to compete, and in this way you can get in some exciting runs with a broader offering of technical terrain and distances. Canicrossers are generally welcomed, although you should be prepared for lots of good-natured jibes along the lines of "that's cheating" or "who's pulling who?" In all situations, it is necessary to act with utmost responsibility, ensuring your dog is under control at all times and does not interfere with the other runners, and that you pick up in the event of a doggie toilet stop. You should be prepared to take full responsibility for your dog's health and well-being during the race and carry a mobile phone in the event of an emergency. A knowledge of canine first aid will give you the confidence to handle any eventuality.

Canicross races are generally

run for the joy of 'taking part' rather than for financial gain – prize purses being generally limited to 'doggy bags', dog food and the kudos of being the fastest team on six legs – or 10 legs if you have two dogs…

EQUIPMENT

Canicross is a great sport that anyone can do and does not require masses of expensive equipment.

HARNESS AND LINE

Because the aim is for your dog to pull out in front of you, a comfortable, padded, well-fitted harness is the ideal. Collars are OK, and allowed, but if your dog is doing any pulling at all, a collar may restrict his windpipe and even cause damage, so a dog harness is your minimum investment.

The harness should be a tracking-style harness that is padded around the shoulders and belly; this is the type recommended by vets. In this style of harness, the line is attached around the centre of the back, so any external pressure is, therefore, nearer your dog's centre of gravity. This might help to minimise any compensatory weight shifting, which may put abnormal strain on soft tissues. Some canicrossers use cross-backed harnesses, but the upward pulling pressure on these harnesses carries the danger of restricting or injuring abdominal or intercostal muscles, or even causing diaphragm trauma, so

should perhaps be avoided.

Most good suppliers will be able to give you sound advice about how to ensure a good fit for your dog. Some outfitters that cater for sled dogs will make bespoke harnesses specifically for your dog, whatever his breed, at very little extra outlay.

Accustom your dog to wearing a harness before starting to canicross. Introduce it gently and calmly, putting it on before something enjoyable happens, such as a mealtime or a play in the garden. In this way, your dog will soon forget about the strange contraption and learn to associate its appearance with pleasant things.

Initially, the attachment to you can be a simple lead. However, if you have a dog that is going to pull, an elasticated, bungee-type lead will allow for a bit of 'give' so that if your dog suddenly lurches forward, you are not going to be swept off your feet. Equally, the jarring to your dog will be significantly decreased and will help prevent the

possibility of injury or strain. The amount of elasticity you need will depend on your dog. Bungee ropes that can smooth out any yanks by holding such energy within the line (such as kinetic-type ropes used for towing) will reduce potentially jarring movements. Care should be taken that your line has some elasticity but does not have too much 'give', as any sudden jerking with the dog snapping back may, in extreme circumstances, cause whiplash-type injuries along the spine, or can accelerate diseased disc degeneration. For this, and other reasons, flexi-leads and choke chain collars are not to be used. Your best bet is to train your dog well so that he is always under control, and exerts just the right amount of pressure on the line.

Most races rule that a line should be no longer than 2 metres (6.5 ft) in length at full extension, but if you are doing this for fun, you can go with what is comfortable for you and your dog.

The harness needs to be well padded.

An elasticated bungee type lead helps to prevent jarring and therefore reduces the risk of injury.

A padded belt will leave you 'hands free'.

A portable water bowl is a must.

Booties made of cordura provide protection if your dog injures a pad.

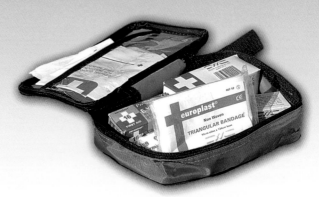

Your vet can advise you on the contents for a first aid kit.

BELT

Many canicrossers are happy holding the lead, but to enable you to run more freely and fluidly, it helps to have your hands free, so a correctly fitting belt that is also padded should also be on your wish list. The padding will make it more comfortable and protect your back from injury, while the 'hands free' facility will help you with your running and balance. Again, there are many types on the market, so shop around and try some out.

RUNNING SHOES

A decent pair of running shoes (without spikes) should be considered an essential.

WATER BOWL AND WATER

You will need a portable water bowl; those brilliant, fabric foldaway bowls are nice and light, and generally available. You also need some water in a bottle that can easily be carried in a bum bag, especially if you are not sure whether there will be access to water on your run, be it a short or long route. This is advisable in order to prevent your dog diving into, and drinking, water that may be contaminated.

By using your own bowl, electrolyte and glucose additives can also be added to your dog's drinking water to give him an instant boost if needed on longer trips. This is recommended by vets for distances of 10 km (6.2 miles) or more.

BOOTIES

Dog booties are also necessary if your dog injures a pad or paw out on the trail, as they will help protect from further damage. Dog boots are protective 'socks' made from a durable material, such as cordura, that fit over your dog's feet and are secured above the ankle or wrist by Velcro. If you condition your dog's feet gently to the sort of substrate that you will be running on, his feet should be habituated to such terrain and he will not need to wear boots all the time.

Dogs cannot sweat like we do and rely on cooling down by panting and, to some extent, losing heat through the pads. Therefore, anything that might impede the cooling process during a run – such as booties – should be used with care. However, a dog that is prone to foot injuries, such as cut pads, might benefit from this accessory. The best advice is to consult your vet as to how to protect your dog's feet on a day-to-day basis. If the terrain is particularly harsh, such as craggy rocks or gravel, wearing dog booties will protect your dog's feet, although sustained exercise on this kind of trail should really be avoided.

It is a good idea to acclimatise your dog to wearing booties before you need them so you do not have a major tussle with a stressed-out dog in a real-life emergency.

POO BAGS

A supply of poo bags will ensure you do not get 'caught short' and will keep you popular with other trail users and the general public.

FIRST AID KIT

A basic human and canine first-aid kit is a must, especially as you progress to longer distance runs. Ask your vet as to what you might need for your dog. Canine first-aid courses are now available and will prepare you for any canine emergency.

WHAT MAKES A CANICROSS DOG?

Most healthy dogs over the age of one year (or 18 months in the larger and giant breeds) are generally ready to run. Dogs and bitches will both be fine for your purposes, although an entire bitch's appetite and attitude for training may be affected by her seasons. A bitch, at a critical time in her season, may also have to be precluded from competing in races for obvious reasons.

If you were choosing a dog specifically for competitive canicross, then athletic, small to medium-sized working breeds will excel. Canicross probably began with the Siberian Husky, which has plenty of energy and, if from good, working stock, will have the confidence and propensity for running out in

The Siberian Husky was born to run and makes a great canicross dog.

A lean, athletic breed, such as the Dobermann, will thrive on the mental and physical stimulation of canicross.

The Border Collie is seemingly tireless and will run until you drop!

front, making the job of training quite easy. Pastoral and gundog breeds, such as Pointers, Border Collies, Springer Spaniels and Labrador Retrievers from working lines, will generally do well, but every sort of breed or crossbreed in between can give it a go. I have known Poodles, Rottweilers and smaller terriers who enjoy haring around the countryside.

However, training your dog at an early age to pull straight out in front will be essential. It is no good having an energetic collie if he only wants to herd wildlife or

other dogs, or a Springer Spaniel who is only interested in following a scent that will take you way off course! Most dogs can be trained to canicross, but the ideal is a confident, calm dog that is not fazed by other dogs, people or new situations, and who will put his energy into racing rather than getting stressed out by the environment.

The easiest way to achieve this is to get a puppy and train and socialise him from the start. The basics of canicross, such as directional commands, can be

put in place quite early on, without needing to do strenuous running work with an undeveloped dog. Obviously those breeds, such as Pekingese, whose physiology – short nose, short legs, heavy coat – may preclude vigorous and sustained cardiovascular exercise would not be suitable. If you want to get canicrossing straightaway then your adult dog already sitting on your sofa is probably your ideal training partner.

Taking on a rescued dog is also a possibility. The majority of dogs enjoy running and canicross is an ideal mode of exercising a new, untried dog who has yet to be trained in the basics of recall. Canicross can help you bond and build up trust, and will mean you get to know your dog much better than if he is off by himself, seeking out bunnies in the undergrowth. Running as a team will get your dog to focus more on you and your commands. Many rescued dogs who have received minimal guidance in early life will often pull like billy-o, so you often do not need to do a lot of training to get your dog out in front – though teaching control is also a must.

Whatever breed of dog you own, I would advise you to get a full check-up with your veterinary surgeon before embarking on this new venture, and seek advice as to how quickly your particular dog should progress with his running. For longer distances, you should wait until your dog is at least two years old but, again, check with your vet.

ARE YOU READY FOR CANICROSS?

Your health and fitness must also be taken into account before starting canicross. If you have not previously had any running experience, get advice from your GP to make sure you do not do

You need to work out a pace that will suit both you and your dog.

yourself a mischief. If you are not ready to run, you can do some caniwalking. This is called 'canimarche', and will also help get you and your dog used to the equipment.

SETTING A PACE

It is important to go at a pace to suit you and your dog, and to keep it safe for the slowest member or your team. So if you are already very fit but your dog is young and unconditioned, you will have to gradually increase speed and distance at your dog's rate. Too much too soon may not only cause injuries but may become uncomfortable for your dog, and he will not want to run with you in this context.

If your dog is the super athlete and you are a couch potato, you

can go slower and concentrate on getting your dog trained to the canicross commands and ensure you have more control. If necessary, give your dog some off-lead exercise or play first to take the edge off his energy so it is easier for him to focus on the training.

SAFETY FIRST

It is vital that you keep an eye on your dog's body language to gauge his state of mind when running, and to be alert for injuries, illness or overheating. If you know what your dog looks like running when he is fit and happy, you will soon recognise a change from the norm and take action. For example, dogs that are getting tired and/or bored may start to increase their attempts at sniffing. In this situation, assume it is due to fatigue. Back off and give him a break with all thoughts of 'personal bests' forgotten.

Running training should always take place when it is cool. Dogs can quickly overheat, being less able than humans to lower their body temperature quickly. Therefore, you need to try to avoid running in the heat of the day for the most part. If you want to keep running during the summer months then, primarily, go out early in the morning or late in the evening. However, as

Intersperse training with walks where your dog is allowed to 'be a dog' and please himself.

many races take place later in the morning then some conditioning in warmer temperatures will be necessary to help your dog cope with running under these conditions. Approach such training with care, however, as many dogs will run until they drop and overheating can quickly be fatal.

Be alert for excessive, fast panting with a large tongue, as well as uncharacteristic stumbling. If your dog does overheat, you will need to lower his body temperature quickly, applying water on his face and covering him with cold towels and blankets that will need to be continually changed and replenished with cool water. A collapsed dog should be taken to a vet immediately. Talk to your vet about what to do if this should happen so you know how

to cope. But the best advice is to prevent it happening in the first place. Stop running if your dog shows any signs of fatigue and do not assume your dog is playing up or being stubborn.

Never run your dog on a full stomach and allow at least two to three hours before, and after, a run before feeding him. Water, with or without the addition of electrolytes/glucose, should be freely available. A dog that is well hydrated before a run will perform better and may be less likely to go off trail looking for the nearest natural watering hole.

Your dog should always come first. Canicross training can be incorporated into your usual walks, but it is not a good idea to solely canicross your dog. You should intersperse training sessions with plenty of good, old-fashioned walkies where he can

just mooch, sniff and mess about. Choose softer surfaces, such as forest tracks and grass, for running, in preference to tarmac and concrete, as these are harder on your dog's paws and are tougher on muscles and joints. It is OK to do short stretches on road, but canicross should ideally be 'cross-country'. Try lots of different canicross routes and do not always take the same trail. This will keep your dog keen and fresh.

A walking warm-up on the surface you will be running on will allow your dog to acclimatise both psychologically and physically to the ground conditions; it will prime the neuromuscular system, making injuries less likely. Veterinary advice suggests that you warm up and warm down for 10 per cent of the distance you aim to run. A 10 km (6.2-mile) canicross run should therefore begin and end with a gentle walk of around 500 m (about a third of a mile). This will help to minimise the risk of muscle ache and strain, and is especially important when in competition.

HIKE ON! – GETTING THE GO AHEAD

Many seasoned runners are happy with their dog running to heel. This is usually accepted in races as long as you are not physically dragging your dog from behind – a real 'no-no'. The only downside is that a heeling companion, or one who mooches in front of you, may trip you up. You are ahead of the game if your dog already pulls out in front, but

To begin with, the dog will need encouragement to run ahead following a 'friend'.

With practice, your dog will understand what is required, and will have the confidence to run out in front.

it is not an excuse for omitting to lead train. Good control on 'technical' trails, where paths are slippery, steep or difficult to pass, will prevent you being pulled over by your dog and getting injured. While it is not desirable for your dog to have to drag your full, dead weight around the trail, a dog that keeps a light tension on the line ensures that the line is straight and also gives a slight 'turbo boost' when needed, such as on the uphill sections. Getting this gentle tension is the essence of what canicross is all about.

If your dog is not keen to be 'out front', do not despair, as you can train him to do this. Firstly,

ensure your dog is in the mood to learn. He should have plenty of energy but not be bouncing off the walls as though he has not been out for several days. If he is too excited, it will be more difficult for him to focus and learn. Train on a definite path rather than an open field, as this will help to channel your dog forward in a line as opposed to casting around in open terrain.

Running out in front can be a self-rewarding activity for some dogs, but you can train it on command, using other rewards as well. Start your straight-line training by getting someone your dog likes to stand several feet

away in front of you. Hopefully, your dog will want to pull to get to them. Just before the line tightens, give your command for running in an excited tone ("Hike" is a recognised canicross term for 'run on fast ahead'). When your dog reaches your friend but with the line still tight, get your friend to reward him with a small but tasty morsel. Repeat often for several short sessions a day – a couple of minutes at the most. Gradually increase the distance between you and your friend, and ensure your dog is rewarded for heading straight forward without stopping to sniff or for a call of nature.

A clear hand signal and the verbal cue "Gee" tells the dogs to turn right.

The verbal cue "Haw" signals a left turn.

Always use the command and reward well while your dog is learning to pull in front.

If you find your dog losing interest over longer distances, go back to rewarding for shorter distances and only slowly increase the distance you are asking your dog to run. Once your dog is doing this for several metres, practise the same exercise with your friend out of sight but appearing with a tasty treat and later with a food reward laid on the trail. In this way you will not always have to use someone running ahead when canicrossing.

Clicker training can fine tune your training; you can 'click' when the tension is exactly right on the lead – i.e. not loose and droopy, but not so that your dog's full weight is forward and nearly pulling you over – and reward a few seconds later by throwing a treat to your dog. A session with a good, reward-based motivational dog trainer may help you get your timing exactly right. By using a specific command for straight-line training in this way, you should not run the risk of ruining your loose lead training. But if you are concerned, it may be a good idea to only allow your dog to pull you when wearing a harness rather than a collar.

Never get cross with your dog, and always end on a successful, high note. Stop your canicross training and running *before* your dog gets tired so your runs will always have positive associations.

THATAWAY! – DIRECTIONAL COMMANDS

While your dog is learning to run out in front, you can also get going on some basic directional commands that will streamline your runs. Your dog will have learned that "Hike" means 'let's go and get a move on'. Two important commands are those asking your dog to go left and to go right on a trail. By teaching this, you can keep your rhythm going, as you will not be tempted to drag and cajole your dog around corners – and it looks really smart!

You can use any words you like to signify this, but canicrossing has stolen from North American sled-dog mushing commands, so, generally, the word "Gee" is used for right and "Haw" for left. You can teach these very simply by using the word just ahead of every time you turn. This can even be done at home if your dog is following you around the house. Every time you turn right, say "Gee" as your dog follows you, and every time you turn left, say "Haw".

Out on the trail, a gentle vibration of the line to indicate the direction required, a clear hand signal in the right direction, and the command given only once will give your dog the idea

Teach a "Steady" command for times when you need to control pace.

Your dog also needs to learn the "Whoa" command so that he comes to a halt on cue.

of what is required in the first instance. If these are repeated at every junction or turn, you will soon begin to see your dog's ears flick backwards and forwards, waiting for the correct command. There is nothing more satisfying than giving a "Gee" or "Haw" and seeing an immediate response from your dog out in front, and it also helps to build up your dog's confidence en route.

STEADY EDDIE
It is good to give words of encouragement every now and then to liven up the pace or to reassure your dog. However, a continual stream may make your dog lose interest, so make your commands meaningful.

Other training commands that you might need are "On by", which asks your dog to go past a distraction – this could be another dog, wildlife, people or a sniffing opportunity. As stated

earlier, dogs should be given the opportunity just 'to be', but when you are canicross training the "On by" command will ensure that you can keep your pace going. The "Heel" or "Steady" command asks your dog to slow his pace and slacken tension on the line. It is important to train this command when you do not need it, so every time the lead goes loose you can put in the "Steady" word and gently praise your dog for doing so. When teaching both "On by" and "Steady", you should gradually build up the level of distraction. Ask to meet friends at pre-agreed set points out on the trail to act as a distraction or an attraction, so that you have a chance to practise your commands in 'controlled' circumstances.

Finally, the "Whoa" command means 'Stop' and will help if you need to bring your dog to a halt in an emergency without having

to yank on the line or use brute force to control your dog. Practise this at a walk first with no distractions and gradually build up your pace and the level of distraction. By using training that is positive and does not rely on manhandling, you will reduce the risk of injury and ensure both you and your dog's energy is put into canicrossing.

FITNESS SCHEDULE
Once you have got your dog pulling out in front and some of the basics in place, you can begin your training programme. If you and your dog are just starting out, begin a gentle 5-km (3-mile) programme after consulting with your own doctor and your dog's vet.

WEEKS 1 AND 2
Powerwalk/canimarche for a brisk 10-15 minutes on alternate days. Before beginning the session, try to encourage your dog to toilet so

you will have less chance of a 'nature break'. In the beginning, if your dog is easily distracted by other dogs, minimise the possibility of such distractions by going somewhere a bit quieter, but if you do get a distraction, practise your "On by" command.

WEEKS 3 AND 4

Introduce a small amount of jogging into your caniwalking, and extend your outings by 5-10 minutes during these weeks. However, do not add too much too soon into your training regime. It is better to leave your dog keen and wanting more, rather than wearing him out and putting him off the whole canicross idea.

WEEKS 5 AND 6

You should now be able to jog a 5 km (3-mile) route within a 30- to 45-minute time period. Remember to vary your route and do lots of different trails to keep you and your dog fresh and to experience varied terrain – do not forget to practise on hills! Always start any session with a 250-metre (273-yard) brisk walk, then break into a run and end with a 250 m cool-down walk.

Once you have got to this level, you can start to build up your speed by running faster for some sections of your run, practising until you can do the whole route at a faster speed.

There are many ideas in human running magazines that can be

Most canicross competitors run dogs of a similar size, but, with practice, dogs of different sizes can learn to run together.

adapted to canicross, but ensure both of you are up to the job. Canicrossers who already have a fair level of general fitness, but wish to become more competitive, should be able to begin a four- to six-week programme, running at least five times a week at a fair (but not flat-out) pace. A recommended rate would be 75 per cent of the maximum cardiovascular effort for your dog to build up stamina for the distance you wish to train for, such as 5 km (3 miles) or 10 km (6 miles). After four to six weeks' interval training, faster speeds can be introduced. Canicrossers at this level should consult a vet specialising in canine fitness (see link below) to ascertain the correct canine cardiovascular

levels and work out an appropriate fitness programme.

For the super-competitive, veterinary-supervised treadmill work for your dog is also a consideration to give you and your dog an edge, though this should not replace actual canicrossing.

A PARTNERSHIP

Always remember that your dog must come first and ambitions for medals and trophies must be secondary to your dog's health and psychological well-being. Watch your dog closely for signs of physical or mental stress or fatigue, and keep it fun. On some days, you may find that your normally perfect canicross dog just wants to sniff, chase squirrels or mark territory and, if this is the case, I suggest you let him do just that and shelve the training session for the day and let your dog do what he wants to do. Canicross is an equal two-way partnership and your dog's happiness should always be part of the equation.

Canicross provides dog owners with a good excuse to keep themselves and their dogs in shape, and gives dogs an activity that they need and love but is often lacking in our increasingly sedentary society.

Dogs can canicross for as long as they can enjoy it and remain injury-free, and I have known seasoned canicross dogs continue running long distances at the age of at 11 or 12, but it will very much depend on the individual dog and their individual health. Because it is a joint venture, it

Canicross is a competitive sport, but never lose sight of the fact the it should be fun for both you and your dog,

helps you strengthen the bonds with your dog and helps him to focus on you, which may help with other aspects of your training. It is straightforward and cheap to do – and besides, you already have the best personal trainer for the job: your dog!

TERMINOLOGY
- **Canicross:** Running cross-country attached to your dog.
- **Canimarche:** Walking cross-country attached to your dog.
- **Caniteering**: Orienteering attached to your dog.

COMMANDS
- **Hike on:** Let's get a move on!
- **Gee:** Turn right
- **Haw:** Turn left
- **On by:** Keep going straight on without stopping
- **Steady/Heel:** Stop pulling out in front
- **Whoa:** Stop (please!)

CANICROSS KIT
- Dog harness
- Two-metre line/lead
- Human waist belt
- Dog booties
- Water bowl/water

USEFUL CONTACTS
www.canicross.org.uk
Canicross Trail Runners Club website for everyone and long-distance/extreme canicrossers and caniteers.

www.canix.co.uk
Canicross event organisers.

www.canicross.com
For all things canicross in Europe.

www.smartvetwales.co.uk
Sports Medicine and Rehabilitation Therapy Clinic, specialising in phyisotherapy and advice on fitness training, injury and rehabilitation for dogs and other animals.

www.caninetherapy.co.uk
Canine massage therapy for fitness.

Canicross equipment retailers
www.culpeppers.co.uk
www.kisi.co.uk
www.snowpawstore.com

DANCING WITH DOGS

Chapter 5

Would you like to boogie with your Boxer or salsa with your spaniel? Well, if you would, then canine freestyle might be the sport for you. Canine freestyle or heelwork to music is where a dog and handler perform a choreographed routine, set to a piece of music. The beauty of this sport is that it allows you to showcase the bond with your dog through individual trick-type moves. You can construct your routine around your dog's strengths, as there are no required elements. So whether you want to compete or just dance around the kitchen with your canine friend, freestyle is a fun activity to teach your dog.

BACKGROUND TO THE SPORT

Competitions in heelwork to music started in the UK in 1996 with similar events being held around the same time in other countries. The sport rapidly captured people's imagination and the number of competitors increased significantly over the following years.

There are now competitions in many countries around the world and the sport has been featured on a number of television programmes. The internet has certainly helped to promote the sport and it also allows new handlers to find out about competitions in their own country.

HEELWORK TO MUSIC OR FREESTYLE?

In many countries there are two different divisions of the sport, with differing elements. Heelwork to music requires the dog to be in the heelwork positions for a certain duration of the routine. The amount of heelwork depends very much on the organisation that you are competing under, so it is best to check what the amount is, and the heelwork positions that are acceptable, before you enter.

Freestyle or dog dance, as it is known in some countries, is where the dog and handler can perform as many moves as they like close up or at a distance. There are no required moves so the handlers can be as imaginative as they like.

GETTING STARTED

It is always a good idea when starting any discipline with your dog to make sure you have a good level of control. At the very least the dog should be able to sit and lie down, work off lead and be able to come when called. It is also essential that you teach your dog to pay attention to you, as the dog will have to respond to many commands or signals

Your dog will be more motivated if you break up training sessions with play.

during the routine. To brush up on your control training, take a look at the Competitive Obedience chapter in this book.

TRAINING THE MOVES

When watching a freestyle routine, the first thing you will notice is the wide variety of moves performed. Some are relatively simple, such as the dog running around you in a circle, and some are more exotic, such as the dog raising his back leg rather than his front leg on command. No matter what move you are teaching, here are some top training tips:

- Keep all your training sessions very short.
- Reward the dog every single time he completes your chosen

move when you are first training a new move.
- Get the dog to perform the action you require before putting a command to it, as this will speed up learning.
- Make sure you vary the rewards you are using, and break up the session by playing with the dog.
- Above all, give the dog as much help and encouragement as you can when you first start training a new move.

BASIC MOVES

WEAVE

This move is easy to teach, but it can look very effective to the audience when performed in a routine.

- **Step 1**: Start with the dog in the left-hand heel position, and place a piece of food in each hand. With your feet well apart, place your right hand behind your right leg so that the dog can see the food. Encourage the dog to follow the food so that he passes through your legs and ends up standing on your right side.
- **Step 2**: Using your left hand, place it behind your left leg to encourage the dog to pass through your legs from the right side back to the left heel position. As the dog passes through your legs, use the command "Weave", and remember to encourage the dog with lots of praise.
- **Step 3**: Gradually start to stand up and when the dog is confidently weaving through your legs on the command of "Weave". You can now start to walk and weave. Do the same as above except, this time, place your right foot forward of your left and get the dog to pass through your legs. Then take your left foot forward and encourage the dog back through the legs to the left side.
- **Step 4**: Now that you are able to weave while walking forward, you can try getting the dog to weave while you walk backwards or move sideways. Also try placing one foot on an upturned bucket and ask the dog to weave - this gives a different appearance to the move.

WEAVE

Step 1

Step 2

Step 3

Step 4

TWIST

This will be one of your dog's staple moves, and, when performed in conjunction with the handler, it can give the impression of the handler and dog working as a team. Explained below is the anti-clockwise twist, but you can also teach the clockwise twist in the same way – but remember to give it a separate command, such as "Whirly".

- **Steps 1:** Get the dog in the heel position on the left side and place a treat in your left hand. Show the dog the treat and take the dog in a wide, anti-clockwise circle back to the left-hand side and reward him. Make sure that as you lure the dog around you, you keep your hand low and level with the dog's head to prevent him jumping into the air on the twist.
- **Step 2:** Now that the dog is following the treat, we can put the command "Twist" to it as the dog is doing the action. Reward the dog after each twist at the start, making sure he always ends up standing straight on your left side.
- **Step 3:** As your dog gets more confident in the move, start to stand up and also try not to use such a large hand signal.
- **Step 4:** The twist can be used in different ways; here are some for you to try:
  - The half twist is where you walk with the dog in the left heel position, twist the dog and turn yourself in the same direction, picking the dog up on the right-hand side.
  - Distance twisting can be achieved by placing the dog behind a barrier. Start by standing up close to the barrier, ask the dog to twist, and then gradually start to move away from the barrier until the dog is able to perform the twist at a distance.
  - The full twist is where you and the dog turn in the same direction for a full 360-degree turn and then continue forward.

GOING ROUND

The round is a useful link between moves and can also be performed both clockwise and anti-clockwise around the handler. Make sure that you give each direction a different command so that you don't confuse the dog. The following sequence teaches the dog to run round the handler in a clockwise direction, so just perform the opposite to teach the dog to go anti-clockwise around you.

- **Step 1:** Get the dog into the left-hand heel position and have a treat in each hand, or use the dog's favourite toy. Encourage the dog to run around you in a clockwise circle, making sure that you have both feet firmly together, as you don't want the dog to

TWIST

Step 1

Step 2

Step 3

Step 4

GOING ROUND

Step 1

Step 2

Step 3

WALKING BACKWARDS

Step 1

Step 2

Step 3

Step 4

get confused with Weave. Do not ask the dog to run around many times when you start – keep it to just the once.

- **Step 2:** Gradually try to stand up, and, as the dog circles you, start to use the "Round" command. When the dog is confidently running round you, try to phase out the hand signal by using just one hand to get the dog to go round.
- **Step 3:** The next stage is to try to walk forward with the dog in the heel position and then send him round. To make the move look different, you could try to turn the opposite direction that the dog is running around you, or kneel on the floor while the dog circles you.

WALKING BACKWARDS

Getting the dog to walk back in front of the handler is a simple but very effective move. A top tip here is to make sure the dog keeps going back straight from the start, and do not ask for too many steps of walking backwards.

- **Step 1:** Get the dog standing in front of you and hold your hands together in front of you with a treat. Using both hands, place them into the dog's chest underneath his chin. As the dog looks down to follow the treat, he will walk back.
- **Step 2:** Start to introduce the command "Back" as the dog follows the treat, and walk

towards the dog, making sure at all times that he is still straight in front of you.
- **Step 3:** Start to take your hands away from the dog's chest as you walk towards him.
- **Step 4:** Vary how you reward the dog – sometimes give the dog the reward from the hand, and at other times throw the treat behind the dog. By throwing the treat behind, the dog should start to walk back more in the anticipation of the reward being thrown.

If you find it a problem keeping the dog walking straight, put barriers either side of him, which will help to keep him walking straight.

THE REVERSE

Step 1

Step 2

Step 3

Step 4

ADVANCING BASIC MOVES

When you have taught the basic moves, it is important not to get complacent but to try advancing them. Here are a few questions that you can ask yourself, which will help you develop the moves:

- Can my dog perform this basic move with minimal signal?

- Can I perform the move without any obvious reward in my hand?
- How can I vary my body position, e.g. kneeling to make this move look different?
- Can I do this basic move at a different pace?
- What move can I link to this move to make it look slick?

CROWD-PLEASER MOVES

THE REVERSE

This move always gets the crowd smiling. It is basically where the dog reverses or moonwalks backwards.

- **Step 1:** Place the dog in a stand and step over the dog so he is

Step 5

between your legs. Have a treat in your left hand and place this on the side of your left leg.

- **Step 2**: Place your right hand with no food in it on to the dog's chest, and gently push the dog backwards. As he walks back through your legs, show him the treat in your left hand and bring it into your left side.

- **Step 3**: Do the same again, but introduce the command "Verse" as the dog backs through your leg.

- **Step 4**: When the dog is confidently moving backwards through your legs to the left side, you can start to stand slightly behind the dog. When increasing the distance the dog

reverses, take it very slowly. If the dog gets into a habit of turning around to look at you rather then reversing, it can be hard to break.

- **Step 5**: To make this move look really stunning, you should aim to have the dog six feet (1.8 metres) in front of you before asking him to reverse.

65

JUMPING THROUGH YOUR ARMS/OVER A CANE

Step 1

Step 2

Step 3

Step 4

Step 5

JUMPING THROUGH YOUR ARMS/OVER A CANE

Jump moves always go down well with the audience, and this method actually allows you to teach two jump moves at once. A good tip is to teach your dog to jump over an agility jump to get used to the command "Over", which means jump something (see Chapter 6: Agility).

- **Step 1:** Make sure you are on a non-slip surface, such as grass or carpet, and sit the dog behind you. Ask the dog to "Wait", walk away and kneel down. Place one end of the cane in your left hand and place the other end against a wall.
- **Step 2:** Show the dog the reward in the right hand, call him, and throw the treat on the ground when the dog has jumped over the cane. This is very important, as you want the dog to make a nice shape as he jumps. If you reward the dog from your hand, he will tend to flop over the arm and not go on far enough.
- **Step 3:** Do the same, but this time introduce the command "Over" when the dog is just about to jump the cane. As the dog starts to get used to jumping the cane, start to stand up a little but be aware of the top height your dog can jump.
- **Step 4:** When the dog is doing

TOP TIPS

- Make sure the dog is sitting well away from you before you ask him to come forward and jump.
- Do not look through your arms when calling the dog to jump, as you might get a black eye as the dog comes at you!
- If you are using food to attract the dog over, you get to the stage of not having a hand to throw it. So, either get someone to attract the dog or, alternatively, place the treat in a dog bowl, as this will encourage the dog to race on after he has jumped and prevent him sniffing around.

this confidently, you can progress the move so the dog is jumping through your arms. This time place the reward ahead of you and hold both ends of the cane. Encourage the dog to jump over the cane and, consequently, through your arms.
- **Step 5:** As the dog gets more proficient at jumping through your arms with the cane between your hands, you can start to move your hands along the cane so that they are closer together. Gradually move your hands closer until they are next to one another. This is when you can dispense with the cane and just hold your hands together.

TEACHING THE HIGH

Getting a dog to stand on his back legs is not a move that is comfortable for all breeds. You must look at your dog before you start to teach this move and ask yourself is the dog overweight or very large, which would mean that there could be excess weight on the back legs. Never do this move with a dog until he is fully mature, and *never* practise this move more than twice in a session, as it is very tiring for the dog.

- **Step 1:** Have the dog facing you and imagine that there is a tall fence in front of you. Take your hand with a treat in it over the fence and on to the dog's nose. Keep the treat very close to your dog's nose; if it is higher, the dog may jump upwards. Encourage the dog to take the treat, and you should find he comes off the ground with his front paws.
- **Step 2:** Gradually increase the time that the dog will be in the high position, depending on the dog's size and ability.
- **Step 3:** Try to phase out the hand signal so that the dog will go into the high on command only. Now that the dog will perform the move on command, try placing him in other positions, such as behind or in the heel position while performing the move.

TAKING A BOW

Step 1

Step 2

Step 3

TAKING A BOW

The play bow is a natural movement for most dogs; you see your dog doing it when he is playing with another dog. When performing, this is an excellent way to start or finish a routine.

- **Step 1:** Ask the dog to "Stand" in the left-hand heel position, and then kneel down beside the dog. Place your left hand under the dog, just in front of his back legs, with your palm facing down, as this will help to keep the back end up. Also have a treat in your right hand close to the dog's nose.
- **Step 2:** Keeping the treat close to the dog's nose, move it down towards the floor in-between the dog's front legs. If the dog does not go into the bow, place your right leg out close to the floor and encourage him to go underneath it, which will result in his front end going down.
- **Step 3:** As the dog's front end goes down, the left hand should keep the back end up. Now you can tell the dog "Bow" or "Bend" and reward him.

CLICKER MOVES

A clicker can be used very effectively to teach some of the more advanced moves in this sport, as it allows you to mark something with a click that the dog might only do for a split second. If you have never used a clicker before, you will need to teach the dog that the click means a reward. This is very simple. All you need to do is to get some tasty treats and click the clicker and give the dog a treat. Any move in this chapter could be taught using a clicker, but here are two moves that you might find easier using the clicker.

FEET ON AN OBJECT

Teaching your dog to put his feet on an object such as a box can be a useful move and can be used in a variety of ways. Make sure the object has a non-slip top and does not move around on the flooring.

- **Step 1:** Sit the dog on one side of the box, and then stand on the opposite side to the dog. Have a treat in your hand and hold it just over the box, then call the dog to you. The dog should be interested in the food, and, by using the food as a lure, you can get him to place his paws on the box. When he does this, either click your clicker or tell him he is good.
- **Step 2:** When the dog will come forward confidently every time and place his feet on the box, introduce the command "Box" or "On" when the dog is on the box.

FEET ON AN OBJECT

Step 1

Step 2

Step 3

Gradually start to remove the food from over the box so that the dog starts to realise that he is being rewarded for placing his feet on the box.

• **Step 3**: Start to leave the dog further from the box, and also move away from the box yourself. Make sure you always go back to the dog if you are away from him, and reward him on the box. As the dog gets more confident, stand with the dog in heel and have the box a few feet in front of you. Then ask the dog to go on to the box. This is harder for the dog, as he will have to leave you rather than come towards you on to the box.

A couple of tips with this move: firstly, do not worry if the dog tends to stand on the box and push it over. The dog almost needs to do this to realise it will move and to step on it rather then it acting as his personal skateboard!

Secondly, increase the time the dog stands on the box, but never let the dog place his feet on the box and run to you for a treat, otherwise the time the dog stays on the box will become shorter and shorter.

PAW WRAPPING

Step 1

Step 2

Step 3

PAW WRAPPING

This is a fun move where the dog wraps his paw around a cane. It looks great in a routine when the handler crosses his leg in the same direction as the dog puts his paw around the cane.

- **Step 1:** Firstly, teach the dog to give you a paw. This can be done by simply lifting the paw and giving the dog a treat from the other hand. Then place the cane horizontally across the front of the dog and ask the dog to give you his paw. When the dog goes to give you his paw, he should place it over the cane. This is when you need to click, no matter if it is only in position for a split second.
- **Step 2:** Gradually move the cane from the horizontal position to the vertical position. You will need to get the cane very close to the dog's body, so you may need to do some work prior to this step to get the dog used to the cane being near him.
- **Step 3:** When you have one paw wrapping around the cane, you can move on to the other paw. However, it might be better to give this a different command so that you can ask for one particular paw.

CREATING A ROUTINE

Now that you have taught several moves, it is time to start to think about linking them together. When you have taught some moves, it is not as important to practise them individually, but to link the moves so that your routine flows freely. Some moves are relatively easy to connect together by linking them with some heelwork. Here are a few tips for linking moves together:

- Look at the direction in which the dog's body is moving. If he is moving forward fast, it will be very hard for him to stop and adjust his body weight to walk backwards.
- Try not to get stuck in one spot by doing too many static moves together.
- Take things slowly and do not rush into doing too many moves together.
- As you build up the moves you link together, it is important that you still reward the dog during the linked moves so that he never knows whether he is going to get a reward after one move or 10.

CHOOSING MUSIC

Finding the right piece of music for you and your dog can be like trying to find a needle in a haystack. The easiest type of track for the first-time handler to perform to is a simple walking beat. Start by just walking along with the dog in heel, on both sides, while the music is playing and build up confidence. As your confidence grows, you can start getting the dog to perform a move and then carry on walking to the beat.

Here are a few questions to ask yourself when trying to find a piece of music to perform to:

- Can I walk to this music in some way that is comfortable?
- Does the speed of the track suit my dog?
- Can you instantly pick out certain places where moves will fit?
- Will you have marker words or is the piece more of a backing track with no specific places that you have to perform moves on?
- Does the music have a theme that certain routine specific moves (RSMs) can be performed? What will you wear to reflect the music?

Choose music that is going to suit your dog's size and personality.

As a general rule, it is advisable not to use a song sung by your favourite singer, as these rarely suit the dog. Here are a few tips for picking the right song for you and the dog:

- Look at your dog – is he big or small? Try not to choose music that is going to be to heavy for the dog – i.e. big, booming music for a Papillion, where, perhaps, a quieter, classical piece would be better.
- Does the track have changes in beat and energy that allow you to perform static as well as moving tricks?
- Are there any props that you could use to aid the routine and create other innovative moves? For example, using an umbrella in Singing In The Rain.
- Good routines are often centred around a theme, such as a movie soundtrack, which your costume and the moves the dog performs can be linked to.

If you are going to enter a competition, you will also need to make sure that the length of the track is correct for the class. It may be difficult to find a track that is the specific length of time you require, so you may find it useful to edit the track on a computer. There are many programmes available that allow you to speed up, fade out or cut pieces out of your chosen track.

PUTTING IT TOGETHER
Here are a few hints on how to construct a routine to your chosen piece of music:

Work to your dog's strengths, and focus on the moves he finds easy to perform.

- Write the track out with either the lyrics, or write down the time in seconds, at points where the music changes.
- Play the piece several times before you actually start planning the routine. Try to imagine a move with a bit of the music and try it out without the dog.
- If the music has words, these can act as markers, which you can use to know when to change from one move to another.
- Fill in the bits that come to you immediately, then go back and see how you could get your dog into the move, i.e. on the right, in front, etc.
- Make sure that you have different start and finish positions, and ensure the dog will do them reliably.
- Analyse the routine and make sure you have not used a move too many times, as you are being marked for a varied content.
- Remember: the judges will be looking for content, accuracy of moves, and interpretation of music.
- When you have a routine, start trying bits with the dog, as some parts will have to change when you get the dog into the equation. Then plan a route round the ring.

TIPS FOR COMPETING
Entering a show can be a scary prospect, so attend some events and see how the show works. There are often some fun events that you can attend, which will allow you to perform a routine with rewards if you need them. This helps both the dog and handler gain confidence.

ENTERING A COMPETITION
You will need to enter a show in advance, so find out from the

organising bodies when the entries close. For each event you will need to fill in an entry form, which will need to be returned with the relevant entry fee to the show secretary.

BEFORE THE COMPETITION
There are many things that you need to think about in order to be ready for the competition:

- Make sure that you have done your pre-competition training, which means doing the routine with the actual props that you are using and also the costume that you will be wearing.
- In the weeks before the competition, make sure you reward frequently all the moves so that the dog is looking for a reward. When using food, try to have it in a pocket and not in your hand so that the dog gets to know that even if he cannot see the food, he will still be getting a reward.
- Every day in the week prior to the event, walk through the routine on your own without the dog.
- If you are using a prop, make sure you know exactly what you are going to do with it, e.g. place it in the other hand or put it down on the floor.
- The day before the show, make sure that you write a checklist of everything you need: costume, props, food, music, safety pins and sticky tape are always good just in case something goes ping!
- Make sure that you have at least two copies of your music,

Most important of all, keep your cool – and enjoy yourself!

and if it has been cut down from the original CD, bring that along just in case the CD that you have put it on from your computer has a wobbly in the DJ's machine!
- On the day of the show, try not to overfeed the dog. If he is fed in the morning, what goes in has to come out – and, also, how do you feel if you have had a large meal? Would you want to work?

ON THE DAY
Firstly, make sure you get to the competition venue in plenty of time, as you do not want to be rushed into the ring. Both you and the dog need to be as relaxed as possible, so it might be good to take a friend with you to help calm your nerves and be a friendly face. If your dog has not been at the venue before, take him in to get used to it, but *do not* over work it – just let him

have a look around. Here are some points that might make the transition into the ring a little smoother:

- When starting to do any practice, begin with really basic stuff.
- Make sure you find out whether all the competitors are working before you so that your dog is not hanging around for a long time.
- Enter the ring and – most importantly – remember to smile.
- If the dog goes wrong, do not try to repeat the move. Simply recall the dog and give yourself a bit of time. Remember, a weave is a simple move that is a good filler while you remember where you are in the music.
- Most important of all, whenever you are competing – *do not panic!*

AGILITY

Chapter 6

W elcome to the sport of dog agility. The fastest, the highest-octane, active and exciting dog sport in the world. It blends speed, skill, co-ordination, balance, discipline and fitness – and that is just in the handler!

A typical agility course will consist of a dog walk, an A-frame, a seesaw, jumps, tunnels, a tyre and weaves. There is a judge on the course, who will be watching to see if all the obstacles are negotiated correctly and that no rules are broken, which would then incur faults on the dog and handler's score.

The overall principle of agility is for the dog and handler to negotiate the course in the correct order, as numbered by the judge, in the fastest time (by use of electronic timing gates).

There are hundreds of shows held throughout the year, all over the world. In the UK there are at least five or six different agility shows every weekend, each with hundreds of dogs entered. In many countries, agility is recognised as a sport.

In Finland, for example, handlers must carry insurance, as they are considered athletes by the sport's governing body (the Finnish Kennel Club) and these are regulated by broader sports organisations.

Agility is now a worldwide sport, and hundreds of shows are held throughout the year.

This is a sport where all sizes of dog can take part; it is only the height of the jumps that changes.

As long as a dog is registered with the Kennel Club on the activities register, he can compete in agility.

A BRIEF HISTORY

Dog agility is now established across the world. The World Championships attract teams from all corners of the globe. As well as the major nations, agility can also be found in countries such as Brazil, Israel, Iceland, Estonia, Norway, New Zealand and many more.

However, it was the UK that first introduced agility to the world. In 1978, the audiences at Crufts were entertained by a demonstration of a dog's natural speed and agility by negotiating a series of obstacles. The display was so well received that agility quickly became something people wanted to do with their own dogs. By 1979 several dog training clubs were offering agility classes, and, in the same year, the first Agility Stakes competition was held at the Horse of the Year Show, at Olympia, London.

At this stage the only dogs participating in agility were 'large' dogs, with jumps at around 30 cms (12 ins). Smaller dogs could still compete, but the height of the jumps made it difficult for them to compete on an even keel.

There are suggestions that agility first took place several years previous to this. The organiser of the first Crufts demonstration, John Varley, was assisted by a dog trainer called Peter Meanwell, who, it is believed, was witness to an agility show in 1974, using a variety of obstacles at an agricultural show. The equipment used there was a combination of jumps and playground equipment, such as a seesaw.

Once agility was recognised as an official sport in 1980 by the British Kennel Club, a standard set of rules and regulations were drawn up, and the first official agility class was held at Crufts the same year, which was judged by Peter Meanwell himself. This was the Crufts team event, which continues to be held at Crufts to this very day.

The Agility Club was the first official club to be dedicated to the sport of agility. It was founded in 1983 and published the first dedicated agility magazine by the same name. From this point onwards, agility began to spread quickly across Europe and then beyond.

By 1987 competitions for 'small' and 'medium' dogs had also been introduced with more appropriate lower jump heights of 40 cms (16 ins) and 50 cms (19.5 ins) respectively. The heights have now been revised, with large dogs jumping up to 65 cms (25.5 ins), medium dogs up to 45 cms (17.75 ins), and small dogs jumping up to a height of 35 cms (13.75 ins).

It did not take long before agility spread worldwide, and the Federation Cynologique Internationale (FCI) formed a set of agility rules that the majority of its member countries then adopted. This helped standardise all equipment, such as jump heights and distances between obstacles, and also improved the quality of judging and show management.

In recent times, the emergence of unaffiliated shows that choose not to use a Kennel Club licence has also gained in popularity, giving competitors the chance to choose which organisation to run under. America has several organisations that have agility competitions and events held under their own systems, one of which is the AKC (American Kennel Club), for example.

Modern-day agility sees many shows each weekend across the world. The biggest show in the world is the Kennel Club Festival in the UK, which is spread over three days with 20-plus rings each day. There are hundreds of websites and videos on the internet; there are handling books and trainings DVDs for sale; professional agility trainers; seminars, sponsors – and thousands of participants.

GRADING SYSTEM & PROGRESSION

The current World Championships are held under the FCI rules. These rules have a three-tier progression system, classes one, two and three. The UK is unique, as it uses a seven-tier progression system, grades one to seven. This is due to the huge numbers of participants compared to other countries.

The FCI rules dictate that dogs and handlers always start at class one and move up by winning classes and having a record book of all the results that they obtain. A dog can become an Agility Champion by gaining a series of results in class three (often wins but not always if beaten by an existing Agility Champion). These have to be ratified by the country where the results were obtained.

Competition at the highest level is intense with top dogs and handlers negotiating the most complex of courses.

Before a dog can compete in agility, he must be physically fit and have a reasonable level of basic obedience.

Championship status is achievable separately in jumping and agility classes.

The UK uses a points-based progression system up until grade six. However, if a dog wins either three jumping classes or one agility class, he is eligible for progression to the next grade. Once a dog is at grade six, he must win a minimum of four classes, two of which must be agility classes, to move into grade seven. Once a dog reaches grade seven, he is eligible to compete in Championship classes. Three Championship classes must be won, under three different judges, for a dog to be awarded Agility Champion status.

GETTING STARTED

There are many clubs and training groups offering agility training. In fact, agility is one of the fastest-growing sports in the world, with people finding its unique blend of excitement, teamwork and skill a perfect way to enjoy their dog and keep fit at the same time.

A simple search on the internet will throw up tens of thousands of results on Google, but a good place to start is the Kennel Club or governing body of the country you are living in. They should be able to provide you with a database of licensed agility clubs and instructors within your area. However, there are many good trainers and small groups who train agility but may not have a licence from the Kennel Club; this is often simply due to the costs. It is expensive for new clubs to obtain a licence, so don't be put off. All you need to make sure is that the club or group you are joining has insurance and that the trainers compete at a high standard.

Dogs cannot start training agility until they are at least seven or eight months, and at that age they will be learning skills, rather than working with the equipment. Between the age of nine months and 18 months – the age at which a dog can start to compete – the dog will slowly increase the amount of physical exertion that he is doing through his training.

Diet and nutrition should not be overlooked. A higher protein diet is recommended, but it is vital that a dog changing on to a higher percentage protein diet uses up the energy that it will give him. If you do not exercise and work your dog regularly, then an active-dog diet may not be practical, as the dog will channel the energy in other ways. If a dog is kept fit and healthy, and not overworked, it is quite common for him to still be competing at 10 or 11 years old. There are special veteran classes for older dogs at most shows.

TEACHING THE BASICS

Basic agility training can be done with a toy and food. I like dogs to be motivated by play and to be rewarded by doing certain skills, not just following the handler around a series of jumps. Control of your dog is vital, and that should be trained as early as possible. A suitable starting point is basic obedience training, which you can begin with a puppy as soon as he has had his

vaccinations and can mix with other dogs.

Although agility does blend verbal commands as well as physical handling, it is vital – at a foundation stage – to get the dog listening to what he is being told, and not merely watching the handler.

PLAY IS THE KEY

The ability to play with a tug toy with your dog is extremely useful when training agility. However, if your dog is totally food-orientated, this can be just as good. When training basic skills, it helps if you can use a reward that is interactive (two-way play between handler and dog). This is great for building a bond between yourself and your dog. A tug-type toy is the best for this, as the dog needs you to play with him. I prefer not to use a ball or retrieve article, simply because the dog can self-reward with a ball and run around with it on his own. I prefer for the play to be the important aspect that the dog learns to look forward to at the end of each exercise, which is the tugging itself.

Once a dog is fixed on to a certain toy, use this toy as your training toy. I have special toys that are used at competition and special toys that are used at training. These toys are specific to the show and training, so the dog does not have them anywhere else. These then become a symbol of work and concentration, but also fun and play (positive interaction and enjoyment with the handler).

Ideally, play should be interactive between dog and handler.

KEY POINT

When teaching any new obstacles (excluding jumps), it is important to use the obstacle command (often the obstacle name) that the dog will learn to associate with that certain obstacle. This may not seem important at first, but it is vital for teaching obstacle discrimination and decision making (which we will talk about later in this chapter), and it is an essential part of working full agility courses, especially at competition.

TEACHING WAITS

The dog is set up behind a jump with his toy in view. He is commanded to "Wait".

The release command is given and the dog heads for his toy.

The handler waits until the dog gets the toy, before moving.

WAITS

A solid Wait gives you a chance to leave your dog at the starting jump and move into position on the course. You do not want to be chasing your dog down a line of jumps right at the beginning of the course. A solid Wait will also prepare the dog mentally, so that he is in a focused state of mind when starting the course and not over-excited and unable to concentrate.

What is most important is the release command. You can make your dog sit or lie down and place a toy in front of him (use a treat box if the dog is only food motivated), and then gradually move away from the dog, building up the distance between you and the dog, before saying your release command. This is typically "Go" or "Okay". This should be given as a verbal command only, not a verbal and body movement. As a handler, it is very easy inadvertently to give multiple messages to the dog, which results in the dog watching the handler rather than listening for his verbal command. Examples of this can be a dog releasing when the handler remains quiet and moves their hand into the air, or the handler walking away and the dog breaking his Wait.

The Wait should be practised over a simple hurdle jump and then built up to a line of jumps, which gives a greater distance between dog and handler. The toy should always be placed to represent the end of the sequence and, at foundation stage, where the dog can see it (in his eye line). Once the dog is set into his start position, the handler should place the toy the other side of the jump and wait for the dog to begin looking at the jump and toy (rather than at the handler) before giving the verbal release command.

This part of the Wait is crucial. Once the release command is given, the handler should watch the dog go over the jump and reach his toy before starting to move. This helps to teach the dog that he should be listening for a verbal release command and not watching the handler for a release signal.

It is always a good idea to practise the Wait in front of a variety of obstacles so that the dog has an overall discipline and ability to wait, not just in front of jumps, but also more exciting obstacles, such as contact pieces and tunnels. Even with the tunnel obstacle, the same principle applies, and the dog

must always pause to listen for a verbal command before any movement occurs.

JUMPING

Teaching the dog to jump properly is an important process. There are no fixed guidelines for the speed at which you should increase the height of the jumps, although I tend to follow this simple pattern for large dogs:
- 6-8 months: poles placed on the ground (between jump wings)
- 9-12 months: poles between the ground and 35 cms (14 ins)
- 12-14 months: poles at 35 cms (14 ins)
- 14-16 months: poles between 35 cms and 45cms (14 ins and 18 ins approx)
- 16-18 months poles increased at appropriate pace to 65 cms (25.5 ins)

These heights are not fixed. The most important factor is the

dog's welfare and safety. Asking a dog to jump too high, too early, can cause serious damage to body structure and muscle growth.

A dog needs to be taught to jump cleanly over the jumps, without pushing his feet against the poles or hitting the wing of the jump. The easiest way to teach a dog to jump is to make the height of the jump very low at first. This makes it easier for the dog to just jump over the pole, rather than run around or underneath it. It is seen as an achievable goal for the dog, and he will learn to jump over the pole instinctively.

Next to teach is the directional commands. It is a huge advantage if the dog will turn away from you as well as towards you. I use "Back" and "This" as my left and right commands; however, it is does not matter too much what you use; more important is what you teach it to mean.

The dog must jump cleanly, sometimes taking directions in mid-air.

TEACHING DIRECTIONALS

To teach directionals, set up a three-sided box and put the dog in a 'Wait" in front of the first jump.

The dog is given the release command.

The toy is thrown and the dog takes off in the desired direction as a verbal cue is given.

INDEPENDENT DIRECTIONALS

It is easy for your dog to learn to follow your body around to the left or the right. However, what is vital is that we teach our dogs to know instinctively which way to turn without needing a physical guide from us.

My preferred way of teaching this is to stand facing the dog in a three-sided box, and recall the dog towards me. The toy is to be thrown to the right (dog's left) and a "Left" directional given. The dog is now hearing his directional command as normal, but the handler's position does not help the dog know which way he is turning; it is purely the verbal command. This helps the dog learn to turn away from the handler independently. Gradually, I will return to a position alongside the dog and will be able to stand and send the dog left or right. If the dog fully understands his directional

commands, it should not matter where I am stood. Obviously, this will be of use more in the higher grades when the courses are more complex.

The other advantage that independent directional commands will give you is the ability to be able to cross behind your dog at any given point of a course, rather than losing the flow as the dog spins or refuses a jump due to your body movement.

TEACHING THE CONTACTS

The concept of the contact points (seesaw, dog walk and A-frame) is for the dog to negotiate them in the correct direction, and to get at least a paw on to each of the marked 'contact points' at the beginning and end of each of the contact pieces. The contact points were originally introduced to act as a safety measure for dogs. This meant they were

encouraged to approach the contact steadily (to avoid falling off), and, once coming down the other side, they again were encouraged to touch a specific area, which would, in turn, assume a certain element of control for the dogs over the whole contact piece.

POSITION AND RELEASE

In basic terms, the best way to teach a dog to perform a reliable and quick dog walk contact is to teach him a position at the bottom of the dog walk first and back-train from there.

I teach all my dogs a 'two paws on, two paws off' position on the dog walk, A-frame and seesaw. I start this process by placing the dog at the bottom of the dog walk, giving a "Get it" command, and praising him for being there. I want the dog to understand that I am pleased that he is in this position. Once I have given the praise, I will release the dog

The aim is for the dog to get at least a paw on the marked contact point.

to the toy with a verbal release command. The toy is acting as a marker to where the sequence ends.

Handlers must be aware that it is very easy, even at this basic stage, inadvertently to teach the dog to look for a physical body release command, when we want him to listen for a verbal command. This can be done by always moving forward as you give the release command, or by constantly flicking an arm when the dog comes off the contact.

It is vitally important that the dog listens and releases only when he is told. This must be reinforced in the early stages of foundation training. If it is done correctly, you will gain reliable contacts that last throughout a dog's competitive career.

Once I have taught the dog his contact position and release command, I start placing him higher and higher up the dog walk's down plank, allowing him

to move down the contact and into his "Get it" position independently. I will then praise him for being there, and, again, give the release command to the toy. It important to praise the dog when he is in the contact position so he knows he is correct. However, the majority of praise should come once you release the dog and he reaches the toy.

Before I let the dog do the whole contact piece, I will introduce a jump at the end of the dog walk, which the dog will jump once released from the contact point. This helps the dog learn that the toy is not part of the contact method, but merely representing the end of the sequence. Once this is achieved, I can let the dog do the whole contact piece, knowing that he will still assume his contact position without looking for the toy as a guide.

The contact points are the

most common obstacle faulted by judges in competition. This can often be a result of the dogs becoming excited and not disciplined enough to stop in their position. With young or inexperienced dogs, it is a good idea to reinforce the contact areas in competition by waiting a few seconds before releasing the dog. This helps the dog keep his composure and discipline in the competition ring, and should help maintain a reliable contact method.

At the time of writing, my youngest dog, three-year-old Taddymoor Scott, has yet to miss a contact in any competition, simply because I have reinforced the action so many times that it is now instinctive, and Scott has no reason to try any other behaviour except that which he knows.

The seesaw is slightly different because of the tip. It can be very off-putting for a dog if he is taken

TEACHING CONTACTS

The first step is to teach the position on the contact area two paws on, two paws off.

The dog is then released to his toy.

The lesson is repeated, placing the dog progressively higher and higher on the equipment.

The dog is given his cue to get the contact – "Get it".

He is rewarded for being in the correct position

When he is given the release command, he runs to his toy.

Before attempting the whole obstacle, a jump is introduced at the end of the dog walk so the dog learns that the toy is not part of the contact method, but the end of a sequence.

On the release command, the dog moves off the dog walk, and takes the jump to find his toy on the other side.

A dog that has been taught correctly will hold his contact position, regardless of where the handler is on the course.

SEESAW

The same principle of learning the contact position is used with the seesaw – although you made need help setting your dog up in the correct position.

On the release command, the dog runs to his reward.

over the seesaw only to discover that it suddenly moves! My strategy is to back-train from the tipped end first (it is useful to have two people to do this), using the same set of principles as for the A-frame and dog walk. However, the dog is learning to include the tip in part of the method, and will grow increasingly confident about the movement of the obstacle.

WEAVE TRAINING

The weaves is one of the most difficult of the obstacles to teach. In my opinion, it is hard for the dog to see the actual point of the weaves. The appearance of the weaves is a little ambiguous, unlike obstacles such as the tunnel or jumps, where the purpose is quite easy for them to understand. The weaves are different, however, and the actual concept is harder for the dog to grasp.

Weave poles are normally made up of 12 poles on a rigid base. The dog always has to enter with the first pole on his left shoulder and continue in and out of the weaves until the 12th pole. Mistakes will result in the dog receiving five faults from the judge. If the weaves are not completed correctly before the dog tackles the next obstacle, the dog is eliminated.

It is important to practise the weaves on both sides of dog. The reason why this is important is because the weaves, like any other obstacle, can be placed anywhere around the course. However, the dog is still expected to enter and complete the weaves correctly. For the dog to be confident to do this, we need to teach a high level of independence - i.e. we need the dog to be able to weave with the handler on both sides, and even behind the dog.

To teach the dogs to weave, I use a training weave called V-weaves. These open to make a V-shaped channel for the dog to run through. Again, it is a good idea to put a focus point (toy/treat pot) at the end of the weaves to allow the dog to focus on where he is going, which means he is more likely to stay in the full set of weaves. It may be a good idea, at first, to open the weaves very wide so that the dog

Weaving is not a natural skill for a dog, so a considerable amount of training is required.

has a straight path to run down to his toy. This gets the dog used to remaining in the weaves and not coming out from the sides.

Due to the bases being fixed at the centre, the dog learns the spacing between the weave poles and this also helps teach the dog co-ordination and how to stride his feet. Overall, the V weaves, even at a basic stage, can be very useful for teaching the dog good co-ordination and balance.

At a steady pace, the weaves should be brought upright so that the dog is weaving between the poles. Before the weaves are fully upright, I add in a start and finish jump, either side of the weaves in a straight line, so that the toy is, again, put beyond the jump to represent the end of the sequence. With the jumps being on either side of the weaves, it helps the dog understand that he

has to look for and pick up the entry of the weave poles when he has more momentum, such as coming from the jump.

Once a dog is confident at finding his own weave entry, the weaves can become fully upright and the transition can be made from V-weaves to normal, upright weaves. It is important to teach and reinforce that even if the angle to the first pole is not straight, the dog must always enter with the first weave pole being on his left shoulder.

WALL, LONG AND TYRE JUMPS

These obstacles are slightly more novelty features than the regular jumps, but the judges will still mark the dogs in exactly the same way. The wall has easily displaceable blocks on top of it, so the dog must jump it cleanly,

in the correct direction, to avoid a fault. Some dogs have a slight tendency to put their back feet on to the top of the wall and push out, thus kicking bricks out of the wall. If you find that your dog is doing this, place a pole across the wall so the dog sees it more as a jump.

The long jump is a long stretch-type jump for the dog. For large dogs it can be up to a length of 1.5 metres (59 ins) and a height of 38 cms (15 ins). For medium and small dogs, the maximum height and length lowers accordingly. It is a good idea to start with just one or two elements and progress steadily. Like the wall jump, it is common for dogs learning this obstacle to 'paddle' and step on the individual elements. This can be faulted by the judge, so if the dog shows any initial signs of

LEARNING TO WEAVE

The V weaves give the dog a clear channel from the start to the finish where the toy is placed.

A dog that is focused on his reward will head straight down the weave channel.

The dog reaches the end of the weaves to get to his toy.

The weaves are moved closer in by degrees, so the dog learns the weaving action.

WALL & LONG JUMPS

The wall has displaceable blocks on the top of it, so the dog must jump it cleanly.

It is best to teach the long jump in stages, adding elements as your dog grows in confidence.

While a dog is learning, the tyre can be lowered before attempting it at full height.

paddling on to the long jump, a regular jump pole can be placed across the elements. This guides the dog and helps him to jump the long jump correctly (i.e. over the elements).

The tyre jump is the only fixed type of obstacle that the dog has to negotiate on an agility course. The tyre hoop can be lowered, and the dog is taught to go through the centre of the hoop by placing a toy just the other side. The dog may be reluctant at first to jump through the hoop, but by rewarding the dog a few times, he will see that there is nothing to worry about. Plenty of play is a must with some of the more obscure obstacles, but you

will find that once the dog sees the point to the obstacle, there should not be a problem with him understanding what he should do.

OBSTACLE DISCRIMINATION

The variety of obstacles used in an agility course means that as well as the dog having the ability to do all the different obstacles, he needs to be able to choose between obstacles presented to him. The obstacles that draw dogs tend to be the more exciting ones, such as contacts and tunnels. When a dog is faced with several choices, it is preferable for the dog to be able

to react to a specific command rather than relying on the handler to guide him to a certain obstacle.

I teach decision-making and discrimination to my dogs. I like them to feel they can take time to make a considered, correct decision, rather than a rushed, erratic decision based on just what they think is right. For this to be realistic, I need the dogs to know the obstacle commands (which I have been using to teach the various obstacles throughout) and to be prepared to go independently to them.

The best way to do this is to give the dog time and space. I often teach handlers to stand still

There are times when you want your dog to make decisions, even when you are not immediately alongside him.

until the correct decision is made – the dog goes to the right obstacle. Then the handler can run forward and catch the dog up, giving verbal feedback at the same time. If the incorrect decision is made, the hander remains still, not moving forward, but recalling the dog and then resending him with the verbal command. The dog will eventually make the right decision, and it is at this point that the handler can reinforce positively. We are effectively teaching the dog that he has as much time as he needs to make a correct decision, rather than the dog thinking he has to take any obstacle as quickly as he can.

One of the most common discrimination challenges that a judge can set up is a tunnel under a dog walk or A-frame facing the dog as he is sent up the up plank. The tunnel is in the dog's eye line, but if discrimination is taught properly and in the manner we have discussed, then the dog should not feel pressured to do what he sees. He should look for the dog walk or A-frame and take that obstacle, without the handler having to block the tunnel entrance, for example. Obstacle discrimination is a very useful skill to be able to use on more complex courses and will really benefit handlers with quick dogs

who get away from them. We cannot always rely on handling these situations, having a confident and independent dog will make certain courses much easier.

HANDLING AND TURNS
Throughout courses there will be many opportunities where the handler can turn in front of their dog, also known as changing sides. There are two ways of doing this: a front cross and a blind front cross. The term 'blind' is fairly common in agility, although its overall benefit has been questioned over time.

The blind turn means changing in front of your dog by

The handler faces the dog to perform a front cross.

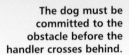

The dog must be committed to the obstacle before the handler crosses behind.

briefly turning your back on him. An easy way of demonstrating this is to stand next to your dog (the dog is on your left), leave the dog by walking forward, and then look over your right shoulder and call the dog to your right-hand side. This process is a basic blind turn, taking the dog from your left-hand side to your right-hand side.

A front cross is similar in what it achieves – the dog changes from being on your left to your right. But instead of turning your back on the dog, the handler leaves the dog on his left, walks forward, and turns in towards his left, facing back towards the dog. The handler continues round and calls the dog and uses his right arm to guide him into his right-hand side. The handler has now completed a 'front cross'.

Once the handler has worked out how to walk through these two types of turns, practising with one simple hurdle jump is the best way to learn timing skills – and for the dog to learn how to read the handler's body language. It is an important skill to be able to use certain turns to

work your way around the course, maintaining flow and speed for both the handler and dog.

The other most common way for the handler to change sides is a 'cross behind', which relates back to independent directions we discussed earlier. A cross behind is useful for when a handler cannot get in front of the dog to perform a front cross or a blind turn. For example, with the dog on the handler's left, the handler sends him on to the jump and crosses behind the jump as the dog goes ahead. As

Agility is a sport that is fun and fulfilling, and keeps you and your dog fit and healthy.

the dog lands, the dog and jump are on the handler's right.

There are many other types of turn and handling systems that can be applied – some are taught by the direction that the handler's feet are pointing – but the basics outlined here will get your through many courses. I have taken four dogs to grade seven (the highest grade in the UK) without using anything but front crosses and cross behinds.

However, I have spent a lot of time teaching the dogs to be confident and enthusiastic to make decisions, to send on to obstacles, to discriminate between obstacles, and to know their contact methods instinctively. When all these things come together, it gives me a huge amount of confidence in my own handling and my own dogs' ability to do each obstacle and course combination.

SUMMING UP

I hope, after reading this chapter, you are inspired to take up the sport, or if you are already competing, you may want to improve and strive to reach higher levels and goals. Agility can give both the handler and dog tremendous fulfilment and enjoyment, and it will also keep you and your dogs fit, healthy, and mentally stimulated.

FLYBALL

Does your dog love to play ball? Do you fancy getting involved in a sport where you and your dog can have great fun and improve your fitness levels in the company of other like-minded individuals? Then maybe flyball is for you!

Flyball is basically a relay race for dogs. Teams of four dogs take it in turns to cross the start line, jump over four jumps, collect a tennis ball from the 'flyball box' and return across the start line with the ball as fast as they can. When racing, two teams of dogs compete at a time, with the first team to complete without faults being the winner of that heat.

Although there are a number of different flyball formats – with variations, for example, in the design of the flyball box and the jump heights used, the basic principles and training techniques are equally valid.

Dogs that are bred to work will thrive on the challenge of Flyball

GETTING STARTED

Will your dog be able to do flyball?

Most dogs should be able to enjoy flyball, and there are lots of different breeds actively competing. There are even multibreed competitions, where all the dogs in the team are a different breed. Flyball is an active sport, though, so your dog does need to be reasonably fit before he starts. In particular, if your dog is one of the very large breeds, or has a long back, I would advise talking to your vet before you start training.

When is a good time to start?

To start formal training it is advisable to wait until your dog is at least 12 months old – you need to be very careful about jumping with young dogs, so talk to your vet before you start. That said, there are lots of fun games and exercises that you can do with a younger pup to prepare for formal training at a later date, which I will describe later.

Do I need to do obedience training before I start?

Different teams will have different requirements. However, you should ensure that you have good control of your dog before you start. In particular, you need to ensure that your dog will return to you reliably when called, even when other dogs are around.

How do I get involved in flyball?

If you are lucky enough to have a team in your area then this is a

Size is not a barrier, as long as your dog is motivated to retrieve.

great place to start. Your national flyball association (see page 111) should be able to help you with this. However, if there is no suitable team in your area, you may need to form your own. If you do need to go down this route, you will probably find that there are teams willing to help you out with information and advice, sharing training sessions or running a training day for you.

WHERE TO TRAIN?

You will need to find a large, flat area capable of accommodating two racing lanes side by side and a reasonable runback area. As a guide, I would recommend a minimum of 100 feet (or 30 metres) in length and 30 feet (or 10 metres in width).

If your training ground is outside, you need to make sure that the surface is suitable for dogs to run and jump on –

thinking about the amount of spring in the surface and ensuring that there are no ruts, holes, etc. in the training area. If your proposed location has a slight slope, bear in mind that you should set up your flyball lanes so that your dogs are running uphill to the box.

If you are lucky enough to find an indoor training ground, again you need to satisfy yourself that the surface is suitable and if you plan to train in, for example, a sports hall, you will need to lay down matting to ensure that your dogs have adequate grip when training.

You also need to bear in mind that flyball can be a noisy sport and not many people like listening to dogs barking for an extended period of time, so there will, ideally, be a reasonable distance between your training venue and neighbouring houses.

Boomerang box

Canadian box.

EQUIPMENT AND LAYOUT
The following equipment will be needed; you will need to check the rules of the organisation that you expect to compete with, to discover specific requirements:

FLYBALL BOX
There are a variety of styles to choose from and the choice is down to personal preference.

What are the main styles available?
The two most common types of flyball box are:
- Boxes with a flat-angled front, which dogs need to trigger to release the ball, with holes situated separately above this.
- Boxes with a curved front, which your dogs need to trigger to release the balls; the holes for the balls are set into this curved area.

How many holes should the box have?
You can get single-hole, two-hole or sometimes even three-hole versions. Which one should you get? And what should the distance be between the holes? The choice is down to your own preference, but these are the considerations you need to take into account.

Many people believe that dogs get a better turn if the holes are offset to the side, and that two-hole boxes encourage dogs to start to turn before they hit the box. Wider holes give more room for larger dogs to get their back paws on the box to push off well. However, other people believe that this encourages too wide a turn, and they are concerned that a dog's paw may get caught in the other hole. Smaller dogs also find it easier to develop a good

turn and, therefore, do not necessarily need offset holes.

JUMPS
As a minimum you will need one set of four jumps. These generally consist of a solid-white baseboard with a width of 24 ins (60 cms) between the sides, which are usually between 24 ins (60 cms) and 36 ins (90 cms) high. The height of the jumps should be capable of being adjusted in one-inch (2.5-cm) increments between 7 ins (17.5 cms) and 12 ins (35 cms). The top of the jumps should be covered with suitable padding; the final jump height will be taken to include this padding.

For ease of reference throughout the rest of this chapter, I will refer to the jump nearest to the start line as Jump 1, the next two as Jumps 2 and 3 respectively, and to the jump nearest the box end as Jump 4.

Flyball jump.

You can select hard or soft tennis balls to suit your dog.

Training Chute.

BALLS

You will also need a good supply of unpunctured tennis balls. If you have smaller dogs in your team, they may find standard-sized balls too big for their mouths and prefer smaller balls or softer training balls. Similarly, as you progress with training, you may find that some dogs perform better with very hard or very soft balls. You will also need two containers to store the balls, for each lane you set up – one at the box end and one at the end of the runback area.

TAPE MEASURE AND MARKING TAPE OR PAINT

To help you mark out the correct position for the box and jumps (and to return them to the correct position if they get knocked over).

JUMP WINGS

Positioned on either side of each jump, these encourage your dog to take the correct line during early training.

TRAINING CHUTE

This is a really useful device for training a good turn on the flyball box. It is basically a large flat board (size) with an impact-absorbing rubber surface, which is capable of being tilted at a series of angles, starting at about 15 degrees from the ground and rising up to a 45-degree angle. Strips of Velcro are attached to the front of the board to allow tennis balls to be attached at a variety of heights.

LANE LAYOUT

A flyball lane is created by setting up the equipment so that there is a distance of 6 feet (1.82 m) from the start gates to the first jump, then 10 feet (3.04 m) in between each jump and, finally, 15 feet (4.57 m) to the front of the flyball box.

PRE-TRAINING

Before you even start formal flyball training, there are some games that you can play with your dog to help lay the foundations for good flyball skills. Do make sure that you treat these as games and keep your play sessions short and fun… with lots of praise and encouragement.

FIND A FAVOURITE TOY

Once you start formal flyball training, it will help if you have already developed a really good bond with your dog so that he is eager to return to you. Finding a motivational aid that your dog

Find a toy that will motivate your dog.

knows and loves before you start is, therefore, a great idea. A long ragger, a ball on a rope, or another toy that you can use to play with your dog is ideal when you come to start flyball training. Treats, balls or small toys can be used, but they have their disadvantages:

Treats can be dropped, causing a distraction for your dog (and the others in the group).

Balls and small toys that need to be thrown as a reward are fine for early training, but when it comes to competition, you will not be permitted to throw anything for your dog in the ring.

PLAY FETCH

At its very simplest level, flyball is a game of fetch. Teaching this early on gets your dog used to the idea that you want him to go away from you to fetch a ball and then return to you. Start by throwing the ball very short distances and keep it fun, with lots of praise and encouragement.

Once your dog can do this, start to hold your dog while you throw the ball and send him away with a command, such as "Go". As your dog starts to go for the ball, turn and run away so that your dog has to chase after you. This is the basis of achieving a fast return from the box.

RETRIEVE BALL FROM ANOTHER HANDLER

Once your dog has mastered fetch, you can try holding your dog and then sending him to

Flyball is basically a game of fetch, and you can train your dog to do this without any equipment.

Your dog will develop quick reactions if he practises catching the ball.

fetch the ball from another handler, who should call your dog and throw a ball up in the air to gain his attention. As your dog approaches, the handler can sweep the ball round in an ark (sometimes to the left, sometimes to the right), encouraging the dog to do a smooth turn, and then roll the ball back towards you for your dog to collect. Now, call your dog and run away, encouraging him to return to you with the ball.

PLAY CATCH

Once your dog starts working with the box, he will need to learn to catch the ball as it is released. Teaching your dog to play catch will help to sharpen up his reactions in preparation for this. As your dog gets better at catching, try to progress to short, fast throws from different directions.

TOP TRAINING TIPS
- Take the training step by step.
- Make sure that your dog is comfortable with the previous step before you move on. If you have any problems at any stage, move back to the previous step and make sure that it is well embedded before moving on again.
- Teach the box and jumps as separate skills.
- This is really important to ensure that your dog consolidates a really good turn before he starts running up to the box to fetch the ball.

Putting the two elements together too early can mean that you end up with a dog that uses the box to stop himself before turning and returning with the ball, which will increase the chances of an injury over time. That does not mean, however, that your dog has to master jumping before you introduce turn training, or vice versa.
- Warm up and warm down. In the same way that human athletes warm up before they start exercising, it is also important that your dog does this, too. In any sport, skipping warm-up and cool-down exercises increases the risk of injury. So you need to ensure that there is an

Teach the box and the jumps as separate elements. This Jack Russell is learning to retrieve from a training chute which has wings to help to guide him to the correct position.

opportunity for your dog to warm up for 5 to 10 minutes before you start any formal training. Examples of warm-up exercises may include a brisk walk or jog around with your dog, gentle ball throwing, a game of tug, or maybe a few repetitions of the 'follow the ball' game described earlier. Similarly, at the end of training session, your dog needs time to cool down again before rest.

- Keep training sessions short and fun. This is particularly important in the early days as your dog learns what is expected and builds up his fitness and stamina. Flyball is an energetic sport… how many times can you run at top speed for 100 metres before you are tired?

- Give plenty of encouragement and reward. Again, this is particularly important when you first start training.

BASIC JUMP TRAINING

You will need to set up a lane of four jumps, with wings on each side of each jump to stop your dog making an error. Some people like to net in the entire lane of jumps at this stage, but I have never found it necessary. I also find that wings are easier to move in and out as you progress to the later stages of training.

Start with the jumps at their lowest height – as in the early stages, you will need to run over the jumps yourself. They can be gradually raised to full height once your dog has grasped the basics.

- **Step 1**: Making sure you have your motivational toy with you, take your dog on the lead over Jump 1 to another handler, who will hold him while you go back over the jump to the start line. Call your dog and run away as fast as you can. Play with your dog when he reaches you.

- **Steps 2-4**: As step 1, but extend the number of jumps, one at a time, until he is coming back to you over all four jumps.

- **Step 5**: Now you can introduce the ball (still no flyball box). Take your dog over the first three jumps on the lead, and set him up facing another handler who is the other side of Jump 4 with a ball. This handler will call your dog and encourage him to come for the ball, gently rolling the ball back towards Jump 4. As you release your dog, turn and run back over the flyball jumps, calling him. Play with your dog when he reaches you. If you have difficulty getting back to the start gate before your dog, it may be worth starting this stage with fewer jumps.

- **Steps 6-8**: As step 5, but extend the number of jumps that you are sending your dog over, one at a time, until he will go out over all four jumps and return to you, holding the ball.

INCREASING JUMP HEIGHT

Once your dog has mastered steps 1-8, you can start to increase the jump heights up to the level that your dog will eventually compete over. Leaving the jumps at too low a height for your dog, for too long, can lead to problems later on with dogs running out, as the height of the jumps in flyball does affect a dog's striding pattern.

I increase the jumps over a period of time – no more than 1 inch (2.5 cm) per training session – making sure that the dog is comfortable at each stage before moving on.

Work at motivating your dog so that he is focused on clearing the obstacle to get to his toy.

REMOVING THE WINGS

At the same time as you start to increase the jump heights, you can also start to remove the jump wings. The speed with which you do this will vary from dog to dog. Some dogs will get the idea very quickly; others will need lots of repetition with the wings as a reminder before they can move on to the next step. As a guide, I tend to remove the wings in the following order – but every dog is different, so you may need to alter the sequence.

- **Step 1**: Remove one wing from each of Jumps 2 and 3; one from the left, one from the right.
- **Step 2**: Completely remove the wings from Jumps 2 and 3.

- **Step 3**: Remove one wing from alternate sides each of Jumps 1 and 4. When doing this, make sure that if your dog turns to the left (as your dog handler looks towards the box) that there is a wing on the left-hand side of Jump 4 (again as the handler looks at the box).
- **Step 4**: Remove the remaining wing from Jump 1.
- **Step 5**: Remove the final wing from Jump 4.

TOP TIPS FOR JUMP TRAINING

- At the start of each training stage, go back to the stage that you achieved at the previous session, thus ensuring that

previous work is consolidated before you move on.
- Do not be afraid to reduce jump heights or put more netting in towards the end of a training session as your dog starts to tire.
- Try to increase the distance from the start-finish line from which you let your dog go… the further back you release your dog, the faster he will be as he enters the flyball lane.
- Make sure that you end the training session on a good note, even if it means taking training back several stages.
- A halfway house to removing a wing is to place it at a diagonal

Progress in easy stages, and your dog will understand that he must jump in a straight line over a series of fences.

at the side of the jump with the edge closest to the jump offset towards the box, and the outside edge offset towards the handler. The wing can gradually be moved out and should act to channel your dog, without forming a physical barrier.

TRAINING THE 'SWIMMER'S TURN'

In my opinion, this is one of the most essential elements of flyball training, and it is well worth putting a lot of time and effort into training this move. The temptation to rush ahead and let your dog run up to fetch a ball from the box may be great. But, left to their own devices and without proper training, a dog faced with a flyball run may develop the habit of approaching the ball head on, and using the box to stop him before catching the ball, turning and returning to

his handler. As you can imagine, this can place a lot of strain on your dog's body and should not be encouraged. Also, it is far easier to teach a good turn from the start than it is to retrain a dog that has a bad turn.

That is why it is important to teach your dog a good turn technique from the word go. This is the basic approach that I take with a dog new to flyball:

PREFERRED TURN DIRECTION

When a dog does flyball, he has the choice of which way he turns as he collects the ball. Most dogs will turn naturally either to the left or to the right. You can gauge this by observing which direction your dog turns as he plays fetch, or when he is retrieving the ball from the 'box loader' in early jump training – this is probably the direction he will choose to turn on the flyball box.

Throughout this section, I will

describe the exercises assuming that your dog naturally turns to the right.

WHAT ARE YOU TRYING TO ACHIEVE?

The purpose of this training is to teach your dog to follow a narrow 'tear drop' shape. Bearing slightly to the left as he clears Jump 4, the dog should then approach the flyball box at a slight angle. He should jump on to the box (still turning to the right), and, as his front paws land, the ball will be released for him to catch while he is still turning. The back legs will then make contact with the box and be used to push off from the box and back towards Jump 4.

TRAINING THE TURN

- **Step 1: Turning on the lead:**
  This exercise is designed to start to embed the motion of a smooth, neat turn before your dog even goes near a flyball box. Start with your dog on your left-hand side with a ball in your right hand, then walk forwards a couple of paces, encouraging your dog to follow the ball. Now turn clockwise on the spot, encouraging your dog to follow the ball until you are facing the opposite direction. Walk a couple more paces, and roll the ball slightly ahead of you for your dog to keep it fun. Try the same thing, starting with your dog on the right.

  As you do this, make sure you keep the ball low so that you do not encourage your dog to jump up at you.

You will find that your dog has a preferred way of turning. This Staffordshire Bull Terrier turns to the left.

This German Shepherd Dog favours a right turn.

- **Step 2: Move this to the chute**: As step 1, but work with the chute set to its lowest possible position, with wings on each side of the chute to prevent your dog jumping off the side. With your dog on your left and the chute directly in front of you, walk directly towards the chute and encourage your dog to turn on the chute.

    Once the basic move has been mastered, try increasing your speed. You are aiming to get all four paws on the chute, with your dog pushing off with his back legs as he goes to retrieve the ball.

    As your dog gets more confident with this, see if you can send him on to the chute – turning without your body to guide him.

- **Step 3: Add a jump**: As step 2, but place a wide jump in front of the chute. This will encourage your dog to jump onto the chute to get the ball, rather than climbing up it. Send your dog over the jump to turn on the chute.

- **Step 4: Add a ball**: Keeping the wings and the jump in place, attach a ball to the chute at the top station, on the right-hand side. Position your dog about 15 feet (4.57 m) away, and get someone to encourage your dog to come and fetch the ball. Then call him back to you and give lots of praise.

    Start with your dog slightly offset to the left of the chute (as you face it), moving over to the right for the recall.

    As your dog gets the hang of this, you can start to release him from directly in front of the chute.

    Then you can add a single jump 15 feet (4.57 m) from the front of the chute, training your dog to go over a jump, collect the ball and return over the jump to you.

    Once your dog is reliably doing this over a few sessions, you can also introduce the chute (complete with wings and jump) into the main flyball run.

- **Step 5: Increase the angle of the chute**: Over a number of training sessions, increase the angle of the chute, first to 30

101

The aim is to get all four paws on the box before pushing off with the back legs.

per cent and then to 45 per cent, making sure that your dog continues to adopt the required turning motion.

As your dog becomes comfortable with this activity, experiment with removing the jump and the wings to see how well embedded the turn motion is.

- **Step 6: Start to reduce the height of the ball on the chute** : At this stage, replace the wings and jump to help reinforce the action that you are trying to achieve. Once your dog is happily jumping on to the chute and executing a good turn with the ball in its lowest position, it is time to transfer to the proper flyball box.

TOP TIPS FOR TURN TRAINING

- Do not be tempted to rush this stage; dogs learn by repetition. Lots of repetition of the correct movement is preferable to failed attempts at a more difficult level.
- You may need to vary the distance between the jump and the chute to encourage your dog to jump on – all dogs are slightly different.
- You may need to help your dog take the right course in the early stages. My preferred method of doing this is to use a piece of angled netting in front of the chute, creating a wide 'entrance' and a narrower 'exit'. I then get a helper to block the exit as the dog

approaches the chute, moving quickly to block the entrance as the dog passes, thus channelling him to take the correct route. If you take this approach, make sure that your dog can always see his objective – a ball.

- Be prepared to treat each dog as an individual. If your dog is not responding to a particular exercise, be flexible and try something else rather than keep going. Remember that what you are trying to achieve is a nice, fluid motion.
- As your dog learns to jump on to the chute, turning properly, you can introduce a trigger command – such as "Turn" – to be given just before the dog jumps on to the chute.

RUNNING AS A TEAM

Flyball is, of course, a team sport, so what other skills do you and your dog require before you can become reliable team members?

PRACTISE WITH DOGS IN THE OTHER LANE

Flyball is a race and dogs need to be able to cope with other dogs running in an adjacent lane without being distracted and running across. This is really important; do not underestimate the damage that even the friendliest of approaches can do to an opposing team's dogs, particularly if a dog is naturally timid.

When you start working with dogs in another lane, include netting down the centre of the runs to minimise the impact on the dog in the other lane if your dog strays.

Your dogs will not always be running in tandem and you will meet lots of different types of dogs when you compete. So, when practising, you need to test how solid they are by releasing your dog at a variety of points before and after the dog in the other lane, trying them out in both lanes and with dogs of as many different speeds, colours, shapes and sizes running against them!

PRACTISE RUNNING WITH OTHER DOGS

Ultimately, you are aiming for the dogs to cross on the start/finish line 'nose to nose', having been released from a sufficient distance from the line to have reached full speed. This is only achieved after many hours of practice, but you need to start somewhere.

- Agree the order in which your dogs are going to run.
- Check which side each dog turns, and make sure that the box loader knows this sequence.
- Line your team of dogs up – with the start dog central, and following dogs fanning behind, to the right of the run as you face it.
- Do not fight over position! If two dogs go from the same point, the first dog to run takes priority with the later dog moving into position once that dog has started.
- As you release your dog, run in towards the line with him, call and then run back, bearing right as you run – away from the dogs waiting to run.

Your dog needs to keep to his lane despite the distraction of running alongside another dog.

You need to work out a running order.

A fast, accurate return, with your dog powering back to you, will keep the team running smoothly.

- Keep your dog under control at the end of the runback area, well out of the way of other dogs until all dogs have run.
- Start with very wide crosses, not releasing your dog until the previous dog is passing yours, and very gradually tighten up. The speed at which the two dogs are approaching each other is very fast, so do not push this too quickly. Make sure your dog is comfortable with what you are asking him to do, and build him up gradually.
- Pick up all your balls!

INTRODUCING THE FLYBALL BOX

You should only attempt this stage when a dog has been consistently performing a good 'swimmer's turn' on the chute for a few sessions. Introduce the box to your dog outside the context of the normal flyball run, in the same way that you did the chute.

Follow the same steps that you did when training the chute, namely:

Turning on the box, on lead. Ball in the box; jump in front of the box – send your dog to retrieve the ball. At this stage be careful if your dog takes a while to learn to catch the ball, as this could interrupt the flow of the turn. Keep the chute training up to reinforce the correct action. Introduce a single jump in front of the box.

Be prepared to be patient and make sure that the turn is reliable before you are tempted to introduce the box to a full flyball run.

ENTERING YOUR FIRST COMPETITION

You will be able to get access to a list of scheduled tournaments through your national flyball association(s), and it is well worth going along to a tournament to watch, before you

are ready to compete. This will give you an idea of the layout and the format of the day. Ask to see a copy of a team registration form so that you know the information you will be required to provide when you start competing.

There may well be Starters Tournaments available. This is a good place to start, as there will probably be training aids in the ring (e.g. wings or fully netted runs); jump heights may be lower than normal, and there may be more flexibility around the rules. These tournaments are a great way to get your dog used to the atmosphere of a competition, without worrying about whether he is 'paw perfect'.

Take note of when entry forms are available, the closing date, and the procedures if the tournament is over-subscribed. These vary from country to country, but entries may be dealt with on a 'first come, first served' basis, so you may need to enter teams as soon as a schedule is issued. (Note: It is usual for a team of dogs to consist of up to six dogs, of which four will be racing at any one time.)

Before the tournament, it is likely that the tournament organiser will issue a running order, stating in what order the divisions will be run, and at roughly what time, and at what time dog measuring will take place. In some countries, the tournament organiser may also allocate ring party duties to teams entering their first team. If this happens and you are unsure, please contact the tournament organiser in advance to warn them – that way they can arrange for someone more experienced to sit with you until you know the ropes.

BEFORE YOU GO ...

- Check what time you need to register your teams – in some places you need to register before all racing starts.
- Make sure that all your team members are registered with the relevant flyball organisation (may not be needed for starters), and that you have their details ready to hand when you arrive.
- Make sure that all your handlers have directions to the venue and ask them to arrive in plenty of time before they need to race. This allows for delays and gives handlers time to warm up their dogs before racing starts. In the case of 'height dogs', they will need to be available for dog measuring.

- Provide all your handlers with your contact phone number in case of problems (and keep your phone with you and switched on).
- Check what the rules are for practising in the ring before racing and/or assistants permitted in the ring (e.g. someone to pick up balls, provide feedback on crossovers).
- Make sure that you have box-loaders and other helpers available as well as dogs and handlers.

ON THE DAY...

- When you first arrive at the tournament, look for the administration area so that you can register your team. The running orders for the day and results should also be recorded here, so that you can monitor the progress of your team.

- Make sure that any 'height dogs' in your team are available for measuring at the appropriate time (not so important for starters, but vital if you enter an open competition).
- Flyball races are usually started with a lights sequence and faults indicated with fault lights or other indicators. Ask someone to explain the process to you and make sure that your team also knows. Generally speaking, the aim is for your dog to be crossing the line as the green light comes on.
- Make sure that your team is ready to race (or available for ring party duties) at the appropriate time.
- Do not forget to pick up after your dog.
- If in doubt, ask! Flyballers are generally a friendly bunch of people and should be more than happy to help.

Find a tournament that is suited to you and your dog's experience.

All team members must have a full knowledge of the rules before the competition starts.

A top team can effect a split-second changeover.

GOALS

TEAM

Different teams have different goals; so whether you are choosing a team to run with or thinking about setting up your own team, it is worth considering what those might be.

For example:
- To be the fastest (not everyone can achieve this).
- To come first in your division.
- To enjoy good close racing, with evenly matched teams.
- To run below a certain time.
- To run consistently, beating faster teams because you run reliably.
- To get the best out of the dogs you have (four dogs can run at five seconds each when timed individually – that doesn't mean the team will run at 20 seconds).
- To make sure every dog, however slow, has a fair chance.
- To run the fastest dogs if needs be to win the race.
- To have fun – all the better if you win.
- To end the tournament placed higher than your seed position.
- To exhibit good sportsmanship, whether you win or lose.
- To enjoy a day out with like-minded individuals, having fun with your dogs.

INDIVIDUALS

Although flyball is a team sport, most flyball organisations include some sort of 'points system'. Dogs accumulate points as they compete in competitions and are awarded with flyball titles as they go through their career – usually starting with the title 'Flyball Dog'.

DOG

Some dogs will have a naturally competitive instinct and enjoy racing the dog in the other lane; others only care about getting the ball and will dawdle back over the jumps in their own time; some even pose for the crowd. Some dogs are super fast and some dogs are very slow.

However, I don't know a dog that cares about world records, first-place rosettes or winning legs… most of them just enjoy flyball for flyball's sake – a fun game to play with their owners as often as they can!

You may have ambitions for your dog, and for your team, but the top priority is to make sure you and your dog enjoy the sport.

NATIONAL ORGANISATIONS

Details of the governing bodies for most flyball competitions in the following countries:

UK
British Flyball Association
www.flyball.org.uk

The Kennel Club also organises an annual knockout competition with eight heats held throughout the year.

USA
North American Flyball Association
www.flyball.org

United Flyball League
www.u-fli.org

INTERNATIONAL
Australian Flyball Association
www.flyball.org.au

WORKING TRIALS

Chapter 8

With very few exceptions the sport of working trials is unique to the United Kingdom, although many of the exercises form part of other disciplines. Trainers such as John Rogerson have introduced trials to parts of the USA, but, in general, people outside of the UK have very little knowledge of the sport and believe it to be akin to Schutzhund. Although there are similarities between the two, they are, nevertheless, poles apart with distinctive differences in both the exercises themselves as well as the emphasis and judging.

That said, there is no reason why working trials could not become popular if there was a spread of information. Trials tests are split into groups consisting of nosework, control and agility, with an option to go on to protection work for those who

want to. However, for owners of breeds that are not naturally suited to 'man work', trials offer an opportunity to make up a Champion in a working discipline without necessarily needing to teach any sort of protection. So, I am hoping that those of you reading this who are not in the United Kingdom and do not want to become involved in Schutzhund, will be sufficiently inspired to find out more about this fascinating sport and perhaps start something where you live.

WHAT IS WORKING TRIALS?

As soon as people hear that I do working trials, they seem to see one of two things: the better informed visualise the big scary scale jump, while those less in the know have a rather vague picture of sheep or guns. Often, when I try to provide a more realistic explanation, their eyes glaze over and I know I have lost

my audience, but, hopefully you will be reading this because you really want to know, so I am not in danger of sending you to sleep!

We must be grateful to the German Shepherd Dog folk for working trials, as it was these breed enthusiasts who originally started the tests as a means of assessing the quality of their dogs for breeding. When GSDs first found their way to these shores it was because of their working ability, which had been proven in combat. Enthusiasts who had seen these dogs working imported them, and were anxious to keep the inherent working ability, good health and construction, which were then so much a part of the breed. It is a shame that many of today's breeders of working breeds do not use the same yardstick.

The tests, as devised back then, have changed very little, and dogs are still assessed on nosework, control and agility and, for those that choose to go further, there is also the option of patrol dog work, which was so much a part of those early tests. Nowadays working trials are for fun, as most of us are not using them to assess our breeding stock. But because of this original intention, it remains the most practical of all the canine disciplines, and is as near as the ordinary person can get to working their dog in a real situation.

As with other disciplines, working trials provides dogs and handlers with a progressive set of tests to enable them to learn as they go along. However, unlike most other sports, there is no requirement in trials to win in order to progress; instead it is all about reaching a standard and qualifying. A long time ago it seems that trials folk decided that it was not necessary to be the best but it was more important to reach and maintain a good level of work, and so, at each stage of competition, handlers are striving to meet a standard and qualify, rather than beat anyone else.

In pursuit of this, each test has a minimum qualifying mark, and there is also an overall qualifying mark for the whole set of exercises at each level, or stake as it is called in trials. Thus, in order to gain the qualification, each test

Does this scary scale conjure up your idea of working trials?

must be performed to an acceptable standard and enough points accumulated to contribute to the minimum overall total. It is not, therefore, possible to qualify with two brilliant sections and one failure, and from this we can see that dogs with working trial qualifications really are all-round working dogs.

Unlike competitive obedience, in working trials you do not lose marks – you gain them. Starting with nothing, marks are allocated in each test according to your dog's performance. Having competed in both obedience and trials, I must say that there is something much more encouraging about gaining points rather than losing them. It is usually possible to get some marks for each test, and so it

makes your dog's efforts worth something, no matter how dismal his performance.

THE STAKES
Trials are divided into different levels called stakes, and each stake is made up of three sections (four in the Patrol Dog stake). These sections increase in difficulty as the dog progresses through the stakes, but the content remains the same: nosework, control and agility with the added Patrol round in the PD stake.

Stakes in working trials are designed to be progressive, allowing inexperienced dogs and handlers to learn at their own pace. With the exception of the Companion Dog stake, all stakes must be qualified at Open level to allow entry into the equivalent Championship stake. To qualify at Open level and gain a Certificate of Merit requires a minimum of 70 per cent of the marks in each section and 80 per cent overall. Certificates of Merit gained at Open trials qualify the team for Championship where 80 per cent of the marks are required to gain the Excellent Qualification at that level.

COMPANION DOG
The first level of trials is the Companion Dog (CD) stake. For this stake you need a well-

THE THREE ELEMENTS OF WORKING TRIALS

Nosework.

Control.

Agility.

behaved, fit and well-constructed dog with some working ability. In CD the emphasis is on control and agility, with only an elementary search and retrieve for the nosework section. There is quite extensive heelwork, both on and off the lead, and at all three paces with no extra commands. CD also includes out-of-sight stays at both sit and down, a recall, and a sendaway.

This is probably all within the reach of a dog working B in obedience, except for what is often seen as the most daunting part of the stake for the newcomers, the agility section, which stays the same throughout the stakes. Although most fit dogs of the working, pastoral or gundog groups will

find this well within their capability, it is often their handlers who lack confidence and convey this to their dogs.

UTILITY DOG

The next step on the trials ladder is the Utility Dog (UD) stake, which is the first tracking stake, and is designed to encourage young dogs and new handlers. The control section has an additional steadiness to gunshot test, but loses the recall and the sit-stay. The heelwork will all be off the lead, and the sendaway will be longer. As with all stakes, the agility will remain the same. A dog that achieves a UD qualification will be an obedient, fit and useful dog that has demonstrated a willingness to work.

WORKING DOG

Following on from UD comes the Working Dog (WD) stake. This is often considered to be the first real tracking test, with more complicated and longer patterns and smaller articles. The search remains much the same as UD although, once again, you can expect more difficult articles, often including smaller, awkward, heavy or metal articles to test the dog. The control section will usually have a longer and more testing sendaway with more accuracy required, and some variation may be introduced into the steadiness to gunshot. Once again the agility section remains the same. A dog with a WD qualification is considered to be just that – a Working Dog – and reaching this level is something to be proud of.

TRACKING DOG

For most people, the Tracking Dog (TD) stake is as high as they go. This is the top level of competition in working trials, and is equalled only by the Patrol Dog Stake, of which more later. To gain a TD qualification, the dog will have to work a much more complicated and older track of numerous legs and intricate pattern. Three articles will be placed on the track and these may be anywhere, although there is always one marking the end of the track. The articles will almost definitely be small and difficult to find, and the track will be marked on accuracy and style. The search square will also have smaller and trickier articles. The

The tracking element traces back to a police dog's ability to find lost people, criminals or evidence.

control section has two additional tests – the speak and the redirect – all this in addition to the usual agility section.

PATROL DOG

For a very small minority of trialists, the Patrol Dog (PD) stake offers a further challenge beyond TD. This stake is optional and very few competitors decide to take this route. To qualify at this level the dog must work the nosework section (which is slightly less testing than that in the TD stake), qualify the control and agility at the same level as TD, and then, in addition to all this, complete the Patrol section (which consists of search, chase and protection exercises and a test of courage). Dogs with either a TD or PD qualification will once again be fit obedient and useful dogs, but with that little bit extra that makes a true working dog.

THE TITLES

At Championship level those gaining 80 per cent of the marks overall will be allowed to add the stake initials plus EX for Excellent after their dog's name, and that is what we are all working for.

For example, Rover CDEX, or if Rover has done very well: Rover CDEX, UDEX, WDEX, TDEX, and even PDEX.

If Rover has been good enough to win a Championship stake at either TD or PD level, he will have won a Challenge Certificate (ticket) and if he does this twice under two different judges, he will be awarded the title of

The Patrol Dog stakes include protection exercises.

Working Trial Champion and also retain his qualifications, so he would become: WT CH Rover CDEX, UDEX, WDEX, TDEX, PDEX – and that is as far as he can go!

THE FORMAT

The exercises in trials have changed very little over the years, which only goes to show how well designed they were all those years ago. Tracking and search squares prove the dog's ability to find lost people, criminals or evidence. The agility section was designed to represent a fence, a ditch and a wall, and thereby demonstrate that a true working dog would not be prevented from doing his job by any obstacle placed in his way, and the control section was to show that the dog was at all times willing and able to do his master's bidding.

Trials take place over several days, and it was not too long ago that competing in any stake meant at least two days at the trial. However, nowadays, when most of the competitors are just ordinary folk and not the ex-military or wealthy retired, it is more usual for all work to be completed in one day in all but the top stake. This means that each competitor completes their nosework, control and agility on whichever day they are drawn to work, and will know at the end of the day whether they have managed to qualify. However, they won't know until the end of the trial whether they are in the places, as it is not until the end of the week when everyone has worked that it is possible to determine the full result. So, in practical terms, you could be drawn to work on the Tuesday, be

TEACHING TRACKING

The handler and dog approach the pole with no knowledge of the scent pattern that has been laid.

A confident start as the Cocker picks up the scent trail.

The handler can give encouragement, but the dog must take the initiative.

lucky enough to qualify, and then find out on the following Sunday that you have won the stake.

Nevertheless, as I have already said, winning and places, while very nice, are not as important as the qualification, and coming home with that precious certificate is what it is really all about. The more important aspect of working on different days is the weather, and it is not unusual in the British climate for it to be raining one day, blowing a gale on the next, and be bright and sunny on the third. This is the true meaning of the "luck of the draw", and when we send off our entries and request a day to work, we have no way of knowing if we will be lucky enough to get the day we ask for, and even if we do,

what the weather will have in store for us.

This is also the case for the two top stakes where nosework is carried out during the week and all those still qualifying come back on the final day to work their control and agility and/or patrol round together. They will all have completed their nosework on different days in whatever weather was prevalent on their day, and it would be very unusual for them all to have had identical conditions. It is funny to hear newcomers to trials declare this as "unfair", as seasoned trialists are quite used to it and accept this as part of the challenge of the sport, even though we all have a selection of hard-luck stories with regard to the day we worked.

UNDERSTANDING TRACKING

After all my talk of tracking, it occurs to me that you may be wondering what exactly a track is, and the truth is that we don't really know. Although many clever scientific people have tried to discover what it is that dogs are able to follow, the closest they have come is to say that it is a combination of bodily scent and ground disturbance. When a competition track is laid, nothing is dragged or put down, other than some articles for the dog to find. It is not necessary for there to be any visible sign of the track in order for the dog to follow it. Obviously, on some terrain (e.g. mud, snow or long grass), the handler can see the track, but

The track ends when the dog finds the article – in this case a toy – at the end of the scent pattern.

The reward – a game with his toy.

this is no advantage to the dog that still follows a scent trail with no regard to visible signs.

To walk a track, the tracklayer does just that – walk. After pushing a pole into the ground to mark the start of the track, he/she will walk the required pattern (which has been designed by the judge and is the same for each competitor), turning as necessary until the pattern is complete. The tracklayer will then leave the track, being careful not to walk over any previously laid part, and allow it to age for the required amount of time. When the handler and dog arrive, they will approach the pole and, with no knowledge of the pattern, will proceed to follow the track, finding articles along

the way (in a perfect world!). Each competitor has new articles and a fresh piece of ground, and tracks are usually laid within an area of approximately 150 square yards.

A straight line of track is referred to as a leg and, depending on the stake, the track can be anything up to 26 or even more legs. Many things can affect a track while it ages, and wind, rain, snow or fouling by wildlife or humans can determine how or if it can be tracked. Terrain also plays a big part, and some grounds track better than others. In the UD stake, the track is left for half an hour before it is worked; the WD is one and a half hours old; the PD two hours, and this increases to three hours for

TD. During this time, any amount of wildlife may have passed over the track, and it may have been rained on or, in frost or snow, it might have thawed out. All of this can affect the quality of the track and make it difficult or even impossible to follow. If the track is failed, it is not possible to qualify overall.

SEARCH SQUARE
In addition to a track, the nosework section also includes a search square, which is designed to ensure that as well as being capable of following a ground scent by tracking, the dog is also able to use the wind to search for his articles. The search square is an area marked out by a steward, walking and placing poles on the

corners, and then placing articles inside the square in whatever location the judge has determined. In CD this area is 15 yards (paces) square with three articles placed, but in all other stakes it is 25 with four articles. Unlike the track, the square is not left to age, and it is worked as soon as the steward has finished laying the articles, although handlers are not allowed to watch the articles go down, so they are not able to direct their dog to them.

Once the dog is sent in to work the square, the handler may encourage and talk to him, and can walk around the outside, but must not enter the square themselves. The dog must retrieve the recovered articles to his handler outside the square, without dropping or mouthing, and deliver them safely to hand inside the time allowed (four minutes in CD and five for all other stakes). The direction of the wind has a bearing on where the dog should be sent in, and handlers can help their dogs by recognising wind direction and sending their dog in accordingly.

Although this exercise does not vary much between the stakes, the size and difficulty of the articles does. Add to this the fact that, like tracks, squares are affected by weather conditions and terrain, and it can be a lottery no matter how good your dog may be.

CONTROL SECTION

The control section is as near as trialists come to working obedience, but I think it fair to say that while the same degree of precision is not required, the tests themselves can be much harder.

HEELWORK

In all stakes, heelwork is carried out at all three paces without extra commands. Although in CD, heelwork is performed on and off the lead, in all other stakes it is always lead free.

I am often told by obedience folk that trials heelwork is terrible, but I can assure you that no marks are lost for good heelwork in trials, and the one or two

Heelwork is not as precise as in competitive obedience, but it should be well schooled and attentive.

THE RECALL

Recall tends to be over a greater distance than in competitive obedience. In this training session, the dog is being held to increase motivation.

On release, the dog accelerates into top gear to reach his handler.

marks gained for smart heelwork can make all the difference to either a qualification or, at the top level, a ticket. It is true to say that trials judges are looking for practical heelwork rather than dressage, and an over-exaggerated or unnatural style in either dog or handler will be penalised, but you can still see some very smart and attentive heelwork on the trials field, and often it is carried out on less than hospitable ground. I think that obedience handlers might be horrified to see the muddy, waterlogged or thistle-covered ground that sometimes serves as a control field, and so heelwork does need to be

practical in order to ensure we stay on our feet! However, it is good to remember that heelwork will be as good as you want it to be, and when striving for a qualifier, every mark counts.

RECALL

The recall only comes in CD and is much the same as a novice recall in obedience, with the one difference that it is usually over a much bigger distance. The accuracy of the present and finish will not be as stringently marked, but a failure to wait or a refusal to come will be heavily penalised. The aim is for a smart, willing and enthusiastic performance.

SENDAWAY

For a trials sendaway, the dog must really want to go and enjoy running. According to the rules, the minimum distance for this exercise is 20 yards (18 m) in CD and 50 yards (45 m) for all other stakes. In reality, it is rarely less than 30 yards (27 m) and can often be 150 yards (137 m) or more in TD and PD, so it is essential that your dog wants to run.

The target for a trials sendaway is whatever takes the judge's eye, and can be anything from a tree or bush to a pylon or tuft of grass, but it will nearly always be some sort of natural feature and

SENDAWAY

The sendaway is a long distance exercise where the dog must focus on a distant, designated target.

The dog must have the confidence to run out while his handler remains in a stationery position.

The target is now close at hand.

The judges are looking for clean drop on the target area.

Finally, the dog is recalled by the handler and must return at speed without deviation.

not a marked-out box or cone. So as far as the dog is concerned, it really is a sendaway and not a 'send to'. In TD and PD this is followed up by a redirect, which, once again, is down to the judge's imagination and can consist of just one redirect or several. The art to this is to teach your dog to go happily from point to point just for fun, so it is important that this, like everything else we teach in trials, is a reward-based exercise.

Firm, fair and reward-based methods should be used in teaching all control exercises to avoid getting a flat, bored or unwilling dog and the ideal is to convince your dog that you are letting him do the exercises rather than asking him to do them. This is a subtle but important difference and, I believe, the basis for the best sort of motivation.

AGILITY

Once again, motivation and attitude are important requirements for the agility section, along with good construction and fitness. Although in CD and UD there are concessions on the jumps for small breeds, they remain at full size for the higher stakes and thus the small breeds are not able to compete at this level.

For the clear and long jump, the dog is sent over, but the handler must not touch or pass any part of the jump, and the dog must remain on the other side of the jump under control until joined by his handler on the command of judge or steward. For the scale, the dog must be sent over, and wait in a pre-determined position until recalled on the handler's command as directed by the judge or steward.

In trials agility, great emphasis is placed on control and all jumps are treated with respect, with no wildness or running at the jumps, which comes as a bit of a surprise to those people who have been competing in pure agility competitions. All the jumps are well within the capability of any fit, well-constructed dog of an appropriate size. Problems are encountered when dogs have hereditary defects, are overweight, or unfit, or when handlers are frightened of the jumps.

CLEAR JUMP

The dog must jump on command.

He must remain under control on the other side of the obstacle until rejoined by the handler.

LONG JUMP

The long jump must be cleared cleanly.

Again, the dog must wait for his handler to complete the exercise.

SCALE

The dog must use his strength and power to jump to the top of the scale.

The dog jumps from the scale and then sits, remaining under the close control of his handler throughout the exercise.

PATROL SECTION

The patrol round is only suitable for dogs of exceptional temperament. They should be confident, fearless, friendly and well controlled, and unless the dog is well balanced and obedient, any attempt to teach these exercises could ruin his temperament and confidence or, even worse, make him dangerously aggressive.

Exercises in the patrol section consist of a series of tests where the dog is required to find hidden or missing persons, defend his handler from attack, chase and detain a running man, face a formidable test of courage, and recall from a chase on command from his handler. These exercises are aimed at testing the courage, obedience and stamina of the dog (and sometimes the handler), and are the only part of working trials that tends to draw spectators.

Because of the danger of training unsuitable dogs for this discipline, the rules require the dog to be qualified up to Championship WD level before competing in PD, and so this guards against macho handlers coming out and setting untrained dogs on all and sundry. Training a PD dog takes a lot of dedication, extra work and, most of all, an awareness of the responsibility, and so it is not recommended for new handlers.

Nevertheless, it is extremely exciting and enjoyable to take out a really good PD dog and compete against the unknown, which is what the patrol round is. The judge can dream up just about any situation and test the dogs and the handlers against the surprise element of an unexpected attack, or the sometimes bizarre test of courage, which is limited only by the judge's imagination, although dog and handler safety must always be of paramount importance. Not a stake for the faint-hearted (handler or dog), but one that can be a great deal of fun and result in a terrific sense of achievement for the qualifiers.

GETTING STARTED

Getting started in trials is not easy – I have often likened it to trying to infiltrate a secret society. I do not know why this is, and since I have become involved in trials, I have made a point of holding 'introduction to working trials' afternoons to encourage more

If you are lucky you will find a group of enthusiasts to train with. This class is working on the Sit-Stay.

people to try this fascinating pastime. However, this is not the case all over the country, and it is sometimes very difficult even to find someone who does trials, let alone someone to teach you. I think this may be because, as a sport, we are very much in the minority. It may also be because

trials training is so time-consuming that, between training and trialling, there isn't much time left to help other people.

But we need to recognise that without newcomers coming into the sport, it will die, and we are already becoming dangerously short of helpers at trials, and

entries are also dropping. So if you come to trials prepared to help, as well as take part, I am sure that those of you in the UK will be able to find someone to show you the ropes. If you are based anywhere else in the world, you can look up working trials on the web and I am always willing to help by email (contact me through my website, listed on p125).

There are one or two really good trials training clubs in the UK, but many parts of the country have no training clubs for working trials at all. So I am afraid that it is often a case of 'teach yourself trials', as I did, and although there are many pitfalls to this method and it definitely takes longer, it is possible, and it certainly ensures that you have a thorough grounding.

Unfortunately, the drawback here is that getting training information in written format is also very difficult and trawling the internet is not much more successful. However, in trials, distant training is a viable alternative, and this is how most of the people who train with us have managed to get started. This involves finding a trainer who you like and having a half- or full-day session with them. You then go away with set goals to achieve, and the back-up of telephone or email advice when things do not go as planned. Once the set tasks have been achieved, you go back for another session. This allows people to progress at their own speed with no pressure, and without the added stress of the competition that can be a part of a club atmosphere.

The biggest obstacle to trials training is a lack of land, and unless you own a large estate with several acres of land, you will need to go cap in hand to local farmers and try to explain what you want to do and get them on your side. It is possible, and a respect for their land and a bottle at Christmas ensures continuing cordiality. Once you are at the stage of needing different terrains for tracking and large fields for sendaways, a local farmer will be your best ally, so treat him well! Having said this, there are certainly plenty of successful trialists without this luxury, and many who get up at dawn to track on the park before anyone else arrives and do sendaways on the local football pitch. So if you are determined and resourceful, you will find a way.

However, before all of this, a lot of trials training can be done at home and even indoors, especially with a young pup. Little searches can start in one room and then progress into another, with the pup kept behind the closed door while the articles are hidden. These can then be taken out into the garden and free searching can be learned a long time before a formal square is introduced.

Control exercises, such as presents, finishes, retrieves and stays, are all best started indoors, and if you are on good terms with your neighbours, it is also an ideal place to begin the "speak". Even a few paces of excited heelwork in the confines of the kitchen can build attitude long before a lead is required, and all this is really good for your pup's brain and has the added advantage of tiring him out and ensuring you get some peace and quiet.

Perhaps the biggest difference about trials training is that most of it is done alone, and this often means that you get a stronger bond with your dog. Spending a lot of time out in the countryside, working alone with your dog, can build a closer understanding with him, and also a greater appreciation of your surroundings. Few trialists can walk or drive past a field without mentally assessing its potential for the various trials exercises, and our knowledge of the farming cycle and what grows when is second only to the farmer's.

The other fact about trials, which, depending on your viewpoint, can be either an advantage or disadvantage, is the travelling, as most of us will admit to driving several thousand miles a year in pursuit of our hobby. However, we do see Britain, and, after about 20 years of competing, there are few places that we have not been to. In comparison to other sports, there are not many trials held in each area of the country, and none in some, so we need to travel to compete. Once in TD/PD this also involves at least one overnight stay, which can be expensive. But, once hooked, and in the trials scene, there are lots of options and trialists often stay with each other, camp or even sleep in their cars. Some, like us, make trials into their holidays and instead of a fortnight in the south of France, it's several long weekends in all corners of the British isles.

SUMMING UP

Well, that is what trials are all about, but before I finish, I'd like to quote something told to me by a police dog handler years ago when I first came into trials. I was really struggling to get my head round tracking and not having a lot of success, and told him that I didn't think I would ever enjoy it.

He said, "There is no better feeling than taking your dog to the post, just as the sun is rising, and with no idea of where the track goes and nothing to see, and watching him work it out and take you round. That is the nearest we ever come to being able to track ourselves."

At the time, I confess to thinking he was slightly insane, as struggling across a wet and muddy field with no idea of where I was going was not my idea of fun, but now I know how right he was. What a privilege it is to watch, at close quarters, an animal doing something that is so natural for him and yet so alien to us, and to truly work in harmony with your dog.

USEFUL LINKS

www.workingtrials.co.uk
www.borderdts.co.uk
www.the-kennel-club.org.uk

Working trials is all about spending time in the countryside working with your dog.

VETERINARY MANAGEMENT OF THE CANINE ATHLETE

Chapter 9

Appropriate veterinary management of the canine athlete requires a two-fold approach. Not only must the veterinarian be capable of treating and rehabilitating the injured athlete, he or she must also be involved in preventative medicine and the development of appropriate training strategies to try to prevent injury in the first place.

As with any athlete, training and competing pushes the dog's musculoskeletal system towards its tolerance limits, and it is inevitable that a dog will get injured at some point in his career. How that injury is dealt with is critical in whether the individual can make a return to competitive athletic activity. Therefore, it is essential that an appropriate diagnosis is reached, followed by instigation of an appropriate treatment or

rehabilitation regime. In most cases, rest and non-steroidal therapy is rarely the answer. It will serve only to mask the injury rather than bringing about a repair or facilitate tissue healing in such a way that will allow the injured tissue to cope with athletic activity in the future. Many athletes fail to return to athletic activity or a working life due to a badly managed post-surgical recovery period or inappropriate conservative management regimes.

The most commonly encountered injuries in general include various connective tissue injuries involving the ligaments, tendons and muscles. Fractures are rarely encountered as a direct result of athletic activity, apart from in the racing Greyhound. Depending on the discipline, neck and back pain are also commonly seen, both as a reason for poor performance, and, in

more severe cases, will progress to fore- or hind-limb lameness depending on the primary location.

INJURY PREVENTION

Prior to embarking on a training regime the following must be established:

- Establish that we have a healthy dog
- Understand the basics of developing a training regime
- Understand how the canine athlete responds to training
- Develop discipline-specific training regimes

Studies on sled dogs have demonstrated changes in their blood parameters compared to the population at large. These changes include an increase in their total white blood cell count (WBC) – these are the cells that are involved with fighting disease and responding to stress within

Sled dogs are endurance athletes and major changes can be seen in their blood parameters compared to dogs that compete in other forms of exercise.

the body. A further increase over and above a resting level is seen in dogs' blood sampled after exercise.

A change in WBC levels can indicate a number of issues including:

- Over-training
- Bacterial infection
- Viral infection

Regular sampling can give invaluable advice regarding the individual's immune system. It also allows for steps to be taken to prevent further damage through alterations in the training intensity and/or appropriate drug therapy.

Changes are also seen within the red blood cells (RBC), with a drop in their concentration. This drop in concentration is often the net result of two different causes. Firstly, many athletes (including humans, horses and dogs), when competing at the highest level, will suffer from blood loss though ulcers in the stomach lining. Secondly, during exercise, the total volume of circulating blood increases, thus diluting out the red blood cells. Endurance training in dogs has been shown to increase plasma volume by as much as 27 per cent.

If dogs are exercised when their total red blood cell count is low, then their performance will be affected due to a reduced level of haemoglobin, the molecule that allows oxygen to be transported around the body. When oxygen levels fall, a greater percentage of energy is derived anaerobically, which leads to increased fatigue and muscle pain. If left unchecked, it can negatively impact performance and contribute to overtraining problems.

In the canine athlete competing at the highest level, particularly those involved in long endurance races, it may well be beneficial to regularly monitor RBC levels throughout the season as well as prior to starting training.

ENDOCRINE SYSTEM

Within the body, the thyroid gland is a two-lobed gland that sits on either side of the trachea or wind pipe at the base of the larynx. The hormone produced by the gland affects all organs of the body, and either an increase or decrease in production can have wide-ranging effects. Alterations in the level of circulating hormones can affect:

- Metabolism of fat and carbohydrate within the body
- Oxygen uptake by the body organs – heart, liver, kidneys
- Growth and development of the musculoskeletal system
- Reproduction
- Hair and skin condition
- Activity levels
- Exercise tolerance and pain

Results from human studies have shown that exercise and training can have variable implications on thyroid hormone concentration and function. Many canine and human athletes will have circulating levels of the thyroxine (T4) hormone that are well below normal reference ranges. One study demonstrated levels up to 40 per cent below that of the normal population. This decrease was attributable to an increase in turnover and loss of the hormone from the body, rather than an inability to produce the hormone in the first place.

Training individuals with low levels of circulating thyroid hormone can often be unrewarding and even damaging to the individual, depending on the severity of the deficiency. Again, repeated sampling throughout the season will help to detect the problem in the early stages. This will allow measures to be taken to prevent it reaching a stage where the animal is showing clinical signs, such as extreme exercise intolerance, fatigue and muscle pain.

MUSCLE BIOCHEMISTRY

During exercise, muscle damage can occur with the result that muscle enzymes are released from the muscle cell into circulation. At low levels this is not a problem; however, high levels of circulating muscle enzymes (creatine phosphate – CK and aspartate transferase – AST) can indicate over-training, and, if significantly elevated, out and out muscle injury. Under normal conditions, a moderate elevation of CK should be seen after exercise with a rapid return to normal values within 24 hours. If levels remain high after this time, it can indicate over-training and an increase in the chance of injury.

The aim of exercise is to maximise the energy available for muscle contraction.

WHAT HAPPENS DURING EXERCISE?

During exercise a demand for energy is created. With training, changes in both the cardiovascular system and the musculoskeletal system occur, which allows this energy to be delivered more efficiently, and for a greater proportion of it to be generated in the presence of oxygen or aerobically.

The aim of training is to maximise an individual's capacity for exercise, i.e. maximise the energy available for muscle contraction. Each unit of energy takes the form of a molecule of ATP and, during exercise, rapid and efficient delivery of this molecule to the muscle is essential. Muscle itself can store very little energy in the form of ATP, rather it has to import it from body stores of fat or carbohydrate and convert it in the presence or absence of oxygen.

ANAEROBIC METABOLIS

At the start of exercise or during bursts of high-intensity exercise, there may be very little oxygen around, and the body may have to generate energy through anaerobic metabolism. This allows for energy to be generated quickly within the muscle and facilitate the increase in workload. However, this type of metabolism or energy generation results in the production of lactic acid and muscle pH drops (conditions become acidic). The net result is that the muscle will fatigue quickly and the muscle will feel heavy and painful.

THE HEART AND LUNGS

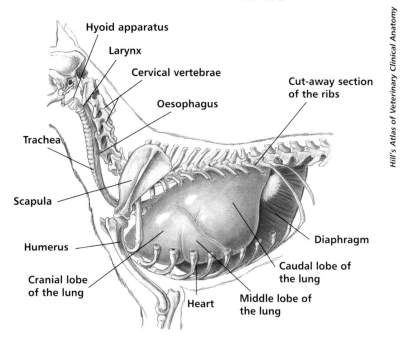

Hyoid apparatus
Larynx
Cervical vertebrae
Oesophagus
Cut-away section of the ribs
Trachea
Scapula
Humerus
Cranial lobe of the lung
Heart
Middle lobe of the lung
Caudal lobe of the lung
Diaphragm

Hill's Atlas of Veterinary Clinical Anatomy

AEROBIC METABOLISM

During low to moderate intensity exercise, aerobic metabolism dominates, which means that ATP molecules are derived in the presence of oxygen. This method of energy production does not result in the production of lactic acid, and conditions within the muscle do not become acidic. As a result, the muscle (and, therefore, the individual) can exercise for longer without getting tired.

In most species, a greater ability to derive energy aerobically during high-intensity exercise is important to maximise performance and reduce fatigue.

ENERGY PARTITIONING

Energy partitioning is the term used to describe the proportion of aerobic to anaerobic energy used during exercise. The higher the proportion of energy derived in the presence of oxygen (aerobically), the better the athlete in general. Little is known as to the interspecies variation in energy partitioning, but it can be assumed that the figure will be very different between the sled dog and the Greyhound. This figure, however, can help with developing an appropriate training programme for a breed and can give us information as to how an individual will respond to training.

In individuals that expend a huge amount of energy in a short period of time, such as the 100-metre sprinter or the racing

Greyhound, most of the energy is produced in the absence of oxygen (anaerobically). Endurance athletes, such as the racing sled dogs, need to have a high capacity to generate energy in the presence of oxygen (aerobically). In other disciplines, such as agility, the majority of the work should be aerobic. When jumping, the energy requirements per second increase dramatically, and an efficient anaerobic delivery is required at this point.

It can therefore be seen that the discipline within which the dog is competing will ultimately determine the training regime, and some breeds may well be more suitable than others for a particular discipline.

THE HEART AND LUNG FUNCTION IN EXERCISE

The heart and lungs or the cardio-respiratory function during exercise is often overlooked during training and rehabilitation.

Cardio-respiratory endurance is the ability of the body, as a whole, to exercise for extended periods of time. When training the heart and lungs, the aim is to improve the delivery of oxygen to the limbs. The more efficient a dog is at doing this, the more energy can be generated aerobically and, therefore, muscle fatigue and soreness is reduced.

Many factors are involved in the facilitation of oxygen delivery:

PATHWAY TO THE LUNGS

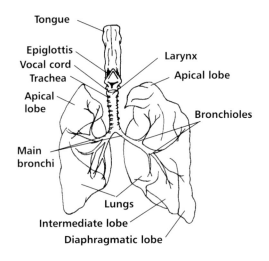

Tongue
Epiglottis
Vocal cord
Trachea
Apical lobe
Larynx
Apical lobe
Bronchioles
Main bronchi
Lungs
Intermediate lobe
Diaphragmatic lobe

- Nostril dilation
- Increase in depth and rate of respiration or breathing
- Increased blood flow to the tissues involved in breathing
- Improved transportation of oxygen around the body

The harder a dog exercises, the greater the need for oxygen. The maximum rate of oxygen consumption or VO2Max is genetically determined and will ultimately determine an athletic ability. With training, an individual can increase his rate and efficiency of oxygen delivery up to this genetically determined limit.

During exercise, the heart rate will increase in line with this increase in demand for oxygen. Every time the heart beats, a volume of blood (stroke volume) is pushed out into the circulating vessels. By increasing the heart

rate and stroke volume, an increase in blood flow to the tissues is seen. Training enables a greater volume of blood to be pumped out to the tissues at lower heart rates.

During exercise also, the amount of blood flowing to various tissues alters. Blood flow to the heart itself, and the muscles of the limbs, is maximised at the expense of blood flow to the internal organs, such as the stomach and intestines. Blood flow to the respiratory system is also increased. Since training can increase the total volume of circulating blood, this results in an increase in the volume of haemoglobin, which carries oxygen around the body. Therefore, a net increase in overall oxygen carrying capacity and delivery to the tissues is seen.

AIMS OF TRAINING

The aim of training is to positively influence exercise physiology to maximise performance.

Training should therefore aim to:
- Improve muscle strength
- Improve muscle endurance
- Improve cardiovascular fitness
- Improve balance and co-ordination
- Increase suppleness and flexibility

Once a basic level of fitness is reached, the demands of each

The racing Greyhound expends a huge amount of energy over a short period.

individual discipline will alter the focus of training. Factors such as age and injury status must also be considered. Ideally, training at the appropriate level should start from an early age.

In the young (skeletally immature) animal, the focus should be on developing balance, co-ordination and proprioceptive awareness (i.e. awareness of the body's position and movement). High-impact, repetitive or high-intensity exercises should be avoided, as they can lead to abnormal loading of the soft tissues, bones and the joint surfaces. The net result is an increased risk of orthopaedic damage or injury to the musculoskeletal system at a later

stage. In general, short-duration, low-intensity and novel exercise regimes, repeated frequently, work the best. In this way, the musculoskeletal system is given time to adapt and develop appropriately in the face of a challenge, and it is therefore primed for when the intensity of exercise increases.

If the onset of training is delayed, however, a crucial window in the development of the neuromuscular system may close and the animal may well never reach his genetic potential. Lack of challenge or limiting exercise to a sterile, flat environment may deprive the neuromuscular system of the challenges it requires to improve

balance, co-ordination and proprioception. Since bones, tendons, ligaments and the articular cartilage all develop in response to the stresses and strains put on them, a lack of appropriate stress can again lead to weaker structures at the end of the day. Delaying the onset of training may also predispose to lack of flexibility in adulthood, which, in turn, may predispose to injury when performing.

TRAINING AND INJURY PREVENTION
The racing Greyhound and the racing sled dog lie at opposite ends of the athletic spectrum. Genetics, as well as training, determine an individual's

An agility competitor needs a combination of speed and strength.

performance at these extremes. The former is the 100-metre sprinter to the latter's marathon runner – and neither is likely to perform well in the other's discipline. Other breeds, however, take up the middle ground, with the majority being more akin to the endurance type of dog in make-up. Agility and flyball require an individual with a combination of speed and strength, while working dogs and those involved in canicross require excellent muscle endurance.

BASIC TRAINING

CARDIOVASCULAR TRAINING
The primary aim of cardiovascular training is to improve oxygen delivery within the body, and to increase the amount of aerobic energy produced. Since it has so far not been possible to determine the maximum rate of oxygen delivery or VO2max in dogs, we have to extrapolate across from human values.

The maximum heart rate (HRmax) achieved during exercise does show variation between species in the dog – from 300 beats per minute in crossbreds to 330 beats per minute in the Greyhound. By extrapolating across from human values, the following figures can be assumed:

- Training at 70 per cent HRmax – 50 per cent VO2max – early-training range
- Training at 80 per cent HRmax – 70 per cent VO2max – moderate- or medium-intensity training
- Training at 90-100 per cent HRmax – 80-100 per cent VO2max – high-intensity training

TECHNIQUES FOR IMPROVING CARDIOVASCULAR FITNESS
- Continuous training
- Interval training

Continuous training: This develops aerobic capacity and involves repetitive whole-body movements, such as walking or running. The aim is to maintain heart rate at a constant level and, ideally, heart-rate monitors should be used. However, these are difficult to use in practice, and, in general, require that an area of coat is clipped over the heart in order to achieve accurate readings. The target heart rate at this stage should be between 60-80 per cent of the maximum heart rate.

A minimum of three sessions a week is advisable initially, increasing to six sessions a week as training progresses. Each session should last for a minimum of 20 minutes, increasing to 45 minutes as fitness levels increase.

Interval training: In interval training, short, repeated sessions of high-intensity activity are alternated with recovery periods of light work. The aim is to work at 85 per cent of HRmax reducing to 35-40 per cent of HRmax in the recovery period. This technique is particularly good for sports such as flyball and agility where short, intense bursts of anaerobic activity are required, over and above a basic aerobic level of fitness.

During this type of training, each individual should work intensively for 30-60 seconds followed by 60-120 seconds of recovery time. This type of

Muscle strength is key for endurance competitors, such as those competing in canicross.

exercise can best be carried out on land or aquatic treadmills.

Circuit training: This type of training may be more applicable during rehabilitation from injury rather than during basic training. It involves rapid movement between different exercise stations and, therefore, requires considerable thought in its design. It is commonly thought of as a way of improving muscle strength and endurance; it can also help improve cardiovascular fitness.

TRAINING FOR MUSCLE STRENGTH AND ENDURANCE

Skeletal muscle will show significant changes in response to training. Whereas the

cardiovascular system responds rapidly to training, changes within skeletal muscle occur much more slowly. Studies in horses have shown that it can take 16 weeks to detect changes within the muscle itself. These changes are mainly associated with the muscles' ability to transport oxygen, and include an improvement in blood supply through an increase in capillary density. One of the other major changes is associated with the biochemistry of the muscle, i.e. how efficiently it can change food substrates into energy.

During training, you should also potentially see an increase in the number and diameter of the individual muscle fibres, which results in a greater muscle mass or bulk. For a muscle to increase in strength, it must be forced to work at a higher level and, unfortunately, many of the techniques employed in human strength training are not feasible in animals.

However, techniques that load the muscle while it is changing length, i.e. during movement, can be used with care, such as pulling weighted sleds or working with resistance bands. The degree to which an overall increase in muscle mass can be achieved will also depend on breed and age. Certain breeds, such as Greyhounds and members of the Mastiff family, have a higher proportion of type I muscle fibres, which are the type of muscle fibres responsible for generating power. It is, therefore, much easier to increase muscle mass in these breeds than in, for example, an Alaskan Malamute or Siberian Husky, which are genetically adapted to have a higher proportion of type II muscle fibres, which are endurance or postural in nature.

The ability to increase muscle fibre numbers decreases with age, so older animals will show a reduced response, and reduced tolerance, to training compared to young, but skeletally mature, individuals.

BALANCE, CO-ORDINATION AND PROPRIOCEPTION

The development of the above are essential, not only to maximise performance in the canine athlete; together, they are the single most important factor in injury prevention. During movement, sensory feedback from the paw/ground contact is integrated with visual and vestibular information within the brain before an appropriate motor response is generated to keep the body upright and moving in the right direction.

The more refined this integration process is, the more controlled and smooth each movement will be and, therefore, the risk of injury is reduced. These skills are not necessarily innate in an animal, but can easily be developed through simple tasks and exercises.

IMPROVING FLEXIBILITY

Flexibility equals the ability to move a joint through its full range of motion without any restriction or pain. It can also refer to the ability of a system of joints to move in a similar way, as in the vertebrae of the neck, trunk and back. When movement in an individual or system of joints is restricted, it can affect performance. For example, tightness in the hamstring muscles will reduce flexion of the hip; this in turn reduces the stride length and therefore reduces speed of movement. Lack of flexibility may also lead to awkward and un-coordinated movement.

Flexibility can be limited by a number of factors:
• Osteoarthritic changes within the joint
• Fat or excessive muscle, which limit movement of individual joints
• Scar tissue
• Connective tissue – ligaments/joint capsule

When considering flexibility, it is important to differentiate between static and dynamic movement. Static flexibility is the amount of movement that a joint can undertake when moved from A to B passively. If the value is reduced, it may lead to an increased risk of injury.

In contrast, dynamic flexibility is the movement generated under the force of a contracting muscle. This is extremely important for determining athletic activity for, as stated previously, any restriction in dynamic flexibility can reduce stride length and therefore speed.

Often, as strength increases, flexibility decreases due to the difficulty in increasing muscle mass, but this is a rarely encountered problem in the canine athlete. Appropriate strength training should result in improved dynamic flexibility.

BASIC TRAINING REGIMES

The Greyhound and the sled dog will have the same basic training requirements in terms of musculoskeletal adaptation. However, skill development should form an important component of the basic training regime. Therefore, since Greyhounds need to be able to corner at high speed, skills to foster excellent balance and develop core stability should be developed from the start.

Irrespective of breed, the following regime should be instigated during basic training:

- Pre-training health check
- Dry and wet treadmill work
- Play
- Motor learning (development of balance, posture and proprioception)

Dogs exercise against the resistance of water when using an aquatic treadmill.

therefore, play can form an extremely important part of training. It can also assist with the canine-trainer bond. By working on different surfaces, such as dunes, grass, or riverbeds, proprioceptive skills are enhanced and such work should also help develop balance and improve co-ordination.

Jogging or free running over different terrain can be a very effective way of progressing an animal through basic training. Ideally, 40-minute sessions, three to four times a week, should be introduced to assist with the development of aerobic fitness. By varying the route and using novel terrain, it prevents boredom and, again, assists with the development of core stability and proprioception.

The dry treadmill provides a secure and constant environment for training. As the days progress, the intensity can be varied through increasing the speed and/or duration, and increasing the incline. It provides a suitable environment for monitoring heart rate, and, as work is on a level surface, it can reduce the risk of injury. It also allows for loading the limbs through the use of harnesses or resistance bands.

In the aquatic treadmill, dogs exercise against the resistance of water. By altering the water level, the intensity of the resistance can be altered. It can facilitate interval training and, again, the load can be increased through the introduction of therabands or weighted jackets.

During training, it is essential that the animal does not become tired or stressed by the regime;

SUB-STRENUOUS/RESISTANCE TRAINING

At this point, high-intensity exercises are introduced gradually. These can further enhance aerobic performance and should progressively increase the load on muscles. Interval training should commence and discipline specific training should start. Techniques to foster proprioception and co-ordination should continue.

Core stability is essential in a situation where a dog works in a crouched position for extended periods.

STRENUOUS INTERVAL TRAINING

Once a basic level of fitness is achieved, further improvement can only be gained through increasing the intensity of the exercise – it is not sufficient to increase the duration of the training session. Again, this is best achieved through intense interval training. Care should be taken to avoid over-training, and the individual should be carefully monitored for any change in health status, behaviour and interaction with others. These can all be early signs of over-training and should be recognised before they progress to disease or lameness.

TAPER

Over the two weeks leading up to a competition, then the intensity of the exercise or training should be tapered off. Ideally, training volume should be reduced by 25 per cent in week one and by a further 25 per cent in week two. The training intensity should remain the same, however.

DISCIPLINE SPECIFIC TRAINING

When building on a basic training regime, the skills required to perform at the highest level within the chosen discipline should be introduced from day one. Agility dogs must be able to manoeuvre at high speeds and, therefore, techniques that focus on flexibility, core strength and proprioception are essential over and above basic aerobic and anaerobic training.

Working sheepdogs must be able to sustain extended periods of exercise coupled with short bursts of explosive speeds. They also spend protracted periods of time in a crouched position or walking very slowly, during which core stability and strength is essential. They are also often working in extreme environmental conditions and may enter a negative energy balance.

Greyhounds, on the other hand, have comparatively low aerobic requirements, rather needing explosive anaerobic release of energy for very short periods of time when racing. It is essential that they learn to corner at speed, and angular stresses must be applied in training to facilitate the development of the bones and connective tissues along the lines of stress.

GUARDING AGAINST INJURY

The fitter or better prepared the animal, generally, the lower the risk of injury. Equal importance should be given during the basic training to the development of both strength and endurance. Avoid over-training by adopting a varied regime and through carefully monitoring the athlete. Introduce discipline-specific training to enhance appropriate responses within the musculoskeletal system for the task in hand. Pay equal importance to the development of proprioceptive skills and core-strength development. Start with appropriate warm-up periods and finish with a cool-down session, and ensure that the athlete is regularly checked by an experienced person prior to, and during, the season.

COMMON CONDITIONS OF THE CANINE ATHLETE

Though all breeds and disciplines are at equal risk of injury, once a dog starts to take part regularly in athletic activity, some disciplines are more likely to result in a certain type of problem. Equally, certain breeds are predisposed to certain types of injury. For example, obedience dogs often show signs of cervical pain and associated forelimb lameness due to the elevated position of the head and neck during training and competition. Low back pain is often encountered in dogs competing in obedience or agility, while traumatic stifle injuries are most often seen in working dogs or agility dogs.

Fractures of the humeral condyles are commonly encountered in the working spaniel while racing Greyhounds are particularly prone to fractures of the metatarsus and carpus.

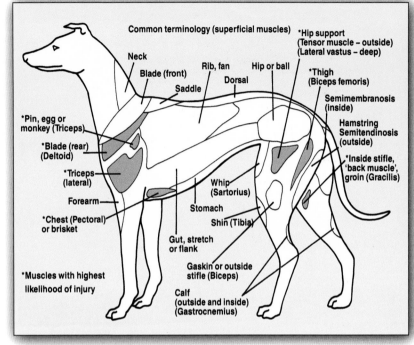

Musculature of the dog.

SOFT-TISSUE INJURIES

BICIPITAL TENDONITIS/TENOSYNOVITIS

This condition is often seen as a cause of intermittent front-leg lameness in sporting dogs, particularly in those involved with agility and flyball.

Diagnosis of this condition is difficult. Often, direct examination of the tendon through the use of an arthroscope is the only way to definitively identify damage to the tendon. However, dogs will be tender on palpation over the point of the shoulder, and will often show discomfort when the

tendon is stretched.

Rest on its own is often unsuccessful as a management option, as it further weakens the surrounding postural muscles. Appropriate rehabilitation and physiotherapy, including the use of therapeutic ultrasound, however, can return a large number of individuals back to competitive work. If such measures fail, surgical management options, which involve sectioning the tendon, should be considered.

CRUCIATE LIGAMENT INJURY OR DISEASE

Damage to the cranial cruciate

If performance starts to deteriorate, it would be wise to get your dog checked over.

ligament is the most common cause of lameness in the dog. Agility dogs are also prone (though far less commonly) to damaging the caudal cruciate ligament as well. The latter may be responsible for a mild hind-leg lameness, which resolves itself after four to six weeks. In the case of cranial cruciate ligament injury, however, the lameness is often severe with the dog reluctant to bear any weight on the limb. It can either happen very quickly, due to injury, or manifests as a long-term, low-grade lameness, which suddenly becomes worse at exercise. Cranial cruciate ligament injury/disease can occur on its own or can be accompanied by cartilage damage (meniscal damage) within the joint.

The function of the cruciate ligaments are to prevent the femur (thigh bone) rolling back on the tibia (shin bone). Damage

to the ligaments leads to loss of stability within the stifle (knee) joint and will lead to osteoarthritis. However, some cases – particularly in small, fit dogs – can respond very well to treatment through rehabilitation and physiotherapy on their own. In general, the best chance for returning to athletic activity is though appropriate surgery on the joint followed by rehabilitation to strengthen the leg and restore proprioception.

Since damage to the cranial cruciate ligament is often a disease process rather than due to a specific traumatic injury, the condition may well occur in both stifle joints.

COLLATERAL LIGAMENT INJURY OF THE HOCK (ANKLE) JOINT
Again, these injuries are most often encountered in dogs that

are turning rapidly, often when landing from a jump. They are associated with a severe lameness during competition and a swelling will be seen around the joint. Management is best achieved through surgery, followed by intensive rehabilitation and physiotherapy.

ILLIOPSOAS MUSCLE INJURY
Damage to the illiopsoas muscle can be responsible for hind-leg lameness in sporting dogs and is often associated with a reluctance to jump or knocking of poles. In general, it responds well to rehabilitation and physiotherapy techniques, which focus on improving the pelvic stability and increasing both strength and flexibility through the low back.

GRACILLIS MUSCLE INJURY
This is the commonest muscle injury in racing Greyhounds. It is associated with a severe lameness that comes on during exercise, and the development of large swellings down the inside of the leg. If the animal is to compete again, surgical re-attachment of the muscle, followed by intense rehabilitation and physical therapy, is the treatment of choice.

NECK PAIN AND BACK PAIN
These can be a common cause both of poor performance and/or lameness in sporting dogs. Recognising the signs can be difficult and the symptoms may often be intermittent. The problem can originate from either the nerve root, the

FIRST AID

As rapid and aggressive intervention is often the best way of ensuring the best outcome from injury, certain techniques employed in the field while waiting for the veterinary surgeon can be beneficial in promoting the animal's recovery.

Ice packs should be found in every first-aid kit. When correctly applied they can help minimise swelling and oedema, and thus help with tissue healing. They can also slow down propagation of pain along sensory nerve fibres and therefore assist with pain relief.

Commercially available ice packs, which are a mixture of alcohol and water, are cheap, effective and easy to use. They should never be applied directly to the skin; rather they should be wrapped in a thin cloth and held in place for approximately seven minutes – any less and they will be ineffective, any longer and they run the risk of causing local burning and increasing, rather than reducing, the swelling.

Simple dressings and bandages to reduce bleeding and to keep the wound clean should also be administered. Be careful to avoid over-tightening any bandage, particularly those that are elastic in nature, as this can irreversibly shut down the circulation to a distal part of the limb.

Rehydration remedies should also be carried, as a means of supplying fluid and energy. During competition many animals are too excited to take in the appropriate amount of fluid and energy. This, coupled with significant losses during strenuous exercise, can lead to metabolic issues as well as dehydration. There are a number of commercially available rehydration drinks that are easily transported, store well and should, again, be an essential part of any first-aid kit.

intervertebral disk, the ligaments and local muscle or the joint capsule. Symptoms can vary from exercise intolerance and a reluctance to complete tasks all the way through to a non weight-bearing lameness of either a front or hind leg. Accurate diagnosis is essential to providing the correct treatment.

Appropriate treatment will vary depending on the severity of the symptoms and the site of the problem, but can extend from painkillers and physiotherapy all the way through to surgery. In general, however, all of these cases will get significantly worse after swimming due to the strain that it places on the neck and back of a dog.

RECOMMENDED READING

Animal Physiotherapy
McGowan, Goff and Stubbs
Blackwell Publishing

Skeletal Muscle from Molecules to Movement
Jones, Round and De Haan
Churchill livingstone.

Rehabilitation Techniques in Sports Medicine
Prentice
Times/Mirror Mosby

Effect of Training and Strenuous Exercise on Haematological Values and Peripheral Blood Leukocyte Subsets In Racing Sled Dogs Davis et al, JAVMA 232; 6:2008 *Alteration in thyroid hormone concentrations in healthy sled dogs before and after athletic conditioning.* Evason et al, AJVR, 65;3:2004.

CONTRIBUTORS

SUE GARNER competes and judges in competitive obedience at the UK's highest level, in addition to training others to achieve their own aspirations with their dogs in the obedience ring, or simply to train a well behaved pet. She undertook her first judging appointment in 1984, and was appointed to award her first Challenge Certificate in 1996. Over the years she has judged in many parts of the UK, Northern Ireland, the Channel Islands and Holland.

For many years she has been a member of Winchester City Dog Training Club, and was the club and show secretary for 15 years. Over the years, her interest in obedience has led to ever increasing involvement in the management of the discipline as a Kennel Club Obedience Liaison Council representative, Accredited Judges Trainer, and giving behind the scenes support to The Kennel Club's Crufts Dog Show Obedience competitions.
See Chapter Two: Competition Obedience.

PATSY PARRY has been training dogs for over 20 years. She has had a go at most dog sports with various dogs that she has owned. She believes in having fun with dogs and dog sports do just that. Patsy has taken part in Rally workshops run by the UK Association of Pet Dog Trainers (APDT).

Patsy runs pet dog training classes in Hampshire, helping owners understand their dogs. She has written and co written three dog training books and runs the education committee for the APDT.
See Chapter Three: Rally O.

NICKY HUTCHISON introduced the sport of canicross to the UK in 2001 and, with musher Matt Hammersley, originally founded Canicross UK to offer dedicated dog running races and to promote the sport. Nicky has a pack of eight Siberian Huskies which she has trained to mush, canicross and do fun agility. When not canicrossing around the Forest of Dean where she lives, Nicky (AKA Weirdwolf) works as a dog behaviourist and for several years has run puppy training classes for Gwen Bailey's Puppy School as well as adult classes and 'obility' (a mixture of obedience and agility). More recently, Nicky set up Canicross Trail Runners with Cushla and Simon Lamen to concentrate on more extreme long-distance canicross adventures.
See Chapter Four: Canicross

RICHARD CURTIS has over 25 years experience training dogs and is one of the leading competitors and instructors in the sport of Canine freestyle/Heelwork to music.

In competitions Richard's dogs have reached the advanced classes in both Freestyle and HTM. Disco, his Portuguese Water Dog made history in 2006 by winning the final of the first Freestyle competition at Crufts. In 2007 Richard then was privileged to be asked to judge all the finals at Crufts.

His winning routines have lead to various appearances on television and at high profile events such as Crufts and Discover Dogs.

Richard is an international judge in the sport and a member of the Kennel Club working party for Heelwork to music/freestyle.

Teaching freestyle has taken him all over the world, having taught workshops in countries such as Australia, Belgium, Japan, Finland as well as many states of the USA.
See Chapter Five: Dancing With Dogs.

LEE GIBSON has been competing and training agility since 1996. To date, he has had four agility dogs and all have reached the top level within the sport. He has also won a medal for Britain at the European Open in 2008. Lee's highly successful team of dogs have taken him to Olympia, Crufts, European Open and many major finals across the UK and Europe. Lee also conducts training and handling seminars around the world, and has also judged at some of Europe's biggest agility shows, including Crufts.

Lee has produced a DVD, the LGT Workshop DVD, which is available from www.leegibsontraining.com.
See Chapter Six: Agility.

BRIDGET LEEK has lived with dogs all her life, but it was only when she got her own dog, Pollaidh (a Border Collie), in 1996 that she became really interested in dog training. Bridget and Pollaidh enjoyed Obedience Training, Agility and Flyball over the years.

They started competitive flyball in 2001 and very quickly got bitten by the bug, particularly enjoying close racing and the camaraderie that they found on the flyball circuit! In 2004 Bridget and her husband Steve formed their own flyball team, with the objective of allowing all team members (and their dogs) the opportunity to enjoy flyball at their own level – be that 'fast and furious' or 'slow but steady' – an objective that remains to this day.

Bridget and Steve have become increasingly involved in flyball over the years; Steve is currently the chairman of the British Flyball Association and together they organised the British Flyball Championships in 2009.
See Chapter Seven: Flyball

WENDY BEASLEY trained her first dog, a Boxer bitch called Sandy at the age of nine, and although not for competition she was a very well behaved dog with a repertoire of tricks, so her interest in training dogs was established at an early age. She went on to work first Boxers and then Border Collies in obedience, working up to Championship level, and then transfered her interest to working trials. Wendy has made up two working trial Champions and won the PD stake at the Kennel Club Working Trial Championships in 2006. She has written two books, one on obedience and one on working trials, numerous articles and is a regular columnist in *Dog World*. Wendy trains both her own dogs, and also helps other people to train their own dogs. After spending time with prison and police dog handlers, she is about to embark on a new venture with her husband Paul,

training dogs for drug detection.
See Chapter Eight: Working Trials

LOWRI DAVIES BVSc MRCVS Cert Vet Acup CCRP qualified as a veterinary surgeon from Bristol Veterinary School in 1992. She then spent several years in Equine practice where she developed an interest in lameness diagnosis and the management of sporting injuries. Her interest then expanded to management of canine musculoskeletal injuries. In 1999 she successfully gained an International Certificate in Veterinary Acupuncture and this was followed in 2005 by a Certificate in Canine Rehabilitation awarded by the University of Tennessee. After a period of further training in the USA she set up the SMART (Sports Medicine and Rehabilitation Therapy) Clinic. The clinic specialises in treating Canine Sporting Injuries as well as trying to provide appropriate, discipline specific training regimes to try and minimise injury. Lowri lectures internationally on canine rehabilitation and management of the sporting dog.
See Chapter Nine: Veterinary Management of the Canine Athlete.

USEFUL CONTACTS

KENNEL CLUBS

American Kennel Club (AKC)
5580 Centerview Drive
Raleigh, NC 27606
Telephone: 919 233 9767
Fax: 919 233 3627
Email: info@akc.org
Web: www.akc.org

The Kennel Club (UK)
1 Clarges Street London, W1J 8AB
Telephone: 0870 606 6750
Fax: 0207 518 1058
Web: www.the-kennel-club.org.uk

The Kennel Club (FCI)
Place Albert 1er, 13
B-6530 Thuin, Belgium.
Telephone: +32 71 591238
Fax: +32 71 592229
Web: www.fci.be

GENERAL TRAINING AND BEHAVIOUR

Association of Pet Dog Trainers
PO Box 17, Kempsford, GL7 4WZ
Telephone: 01285 810811
Email: APDToffice@aol.com
Web: http://www.apdt.co.uk

Association of Pet Behaviour Counsellors
PO BOX 46, Worcester, WR8 9YS
Telephone: 01386 751151
Fax: 01386 750743
Email: info@apbc.org.uk
Web: http://www.apbc.org.uk/

AGILITY

Agility Club
http://www.agilityclub.co.uk/

Agilitynet (UK)
38 Northolme Road, London N5 2UU
Telephone. 020 7359 6461
Fax. 020 7704 1906
Web: www.agilitynet.co.uk

United States Dog Agility Association
Telephone: 972 487 2200
Fax: 972 231 9700
Web: www.usdaa.com

CANICROSS

Canicross Trail Runners Club
www.canicross.org.uk

Event Organisers
www.canix.co.uk
www.cani-cross.co.uk

European Canicross
www.canicross.com

DANCING WITH DOGS

World Canine Freestyle Organisation
P.O. Box 350122, Brooklyn, NY
11235-2525, USA
Telephone: (718) 332-8336
Fax: (718) 646-2686
Email: wcfodogs@aol.com
Web: www.worldcaninefreestyle.org

FLYBALL

British Flyball Association
PO Box 990, Doncaster, DN1 9FY
Telephone: 01628 829623
Email: secretary@flyball.org.uk
Web: http://www.flyball.org.uk/

North American Flyball Association
www.flyball.org

United Flyball League
www.u-fli.org

Australian Flyball Association
www.flyball.org.au

RALLY O

Contact your kennel club for details of organisations in your area.

WORKING TRIALS

Working Trials UK
www.workingtrials.co.uk

Working Trials Training
www.borderdts.co.uk

Association of American Working Trials Societies
www.waggin-tails.com/workingtrials/